MW00888550

The Trials of Mata Hari

Margaretha Geertruida Zelle a.k.a. Mata Hari

By

Jan Bernard Stolz

Copyright ©2024 by Jan Stolz

1

Other books by Jan Stolz available on Amazon:

The Men Who Made the Comics
My Place among the Microbes
Iron-Man of the Sierras
(The Saga of Snowshoe Thompson)
Iron-Man of the Yellowstone
(The life of Mountain Man John Colter)
The Long Way Home
(The incredible survival of Capt. Gordon Manuel)
The Quiet American Hero
(The Real Life of Audie Murphy)
Running Men
(Olympians Louis Tewanima & Jim Thorpe)
Reap the Wild Wind
(John Patterson vs. the Great Dayton Flood)
"The Lost Dutchman" Jacob Waltz
Song of the Poor Clares
(And how it became the Voynich Manuscript)
The Buccaneers
The Story in Stone
The Spring-Heeled Jack
Shadows Past
(The First Lord Baltimore novel)
Dauntless
(The Second Lord Baltimore novel)
Fact or Fiction?
Fact or Fiction? Vol. 2 Vanished!
Galaxy 9
The Family Van Horn

2

The Trials of Mata Hari

Table of Contents

Introduction

WORLD WAR I – The War to End all Wars – was in its third year. The Allies had yet to beat back the German advance. In the Spring of 1917 France was suddenly shaken by the Great Mutinies of the French Army following the failure of the Nivelle Offensive. Many believed the collapse of France was inevitable.

Then, in July, came a new government in under "Le Tigre" Georges Clemenceau. Utterly committed to winning the war, but unwilling to admit the failures of its military leaders, it was decided the most convenient out for the French government was to lay the blame for everything that had gone wrong with the war thus far on a single German spy.

Margaretha Geertruida Zelle, a.k.a., the ill reputed Mata Hari, became the perfect scapegoat.

This is her story.

At La Scala in Milan - 1912

This book is a Novelization of
Actual events that took place
Between 1876 – 1917

The events really happened, with
Only occasional dialog being fictional.

What does a government do when they realize
They have executed an innocent person?
Cover it up, of course.

Mata-Hari débarquant à Gijon
(Espagne) en novembre 1916,
où l'attendait un agent chargé
de la surveiller.

Chapter 1

"You – I will grind into dust!"

❖   ❖   ❖

February 13, 1917

ON THIS GREY winter morning, Paris Police Commissioner Albert Priolet, arrest warrant in hand, entered the lobby of the glamourous Élysées Palace Hotel accompanied by five inspectors. Flashing his badge and credentials at the clerks behind the check-in counter as he passed, the group of men made their way to the elevator.

Pausing as they waited for the lift cage to descend to the ground floor, Priolet glanced at the other officers.

"You two – come with me." He said, pointing out his choices. "You other three take the stairs. Third floor. I want to make sure she doesn't slip by us."

The three officers nodded then headed for the stairs.

THE ELEVATOR DOORS opened onto the third floor landing. Priolet and the two officers stepped out of the lift just as the other men topped the stairwell. His group intact once again, Priolet proceeded down the elegant hallway, his officers following close on his heels.

Stopping before one of the rooms, Priolet rapped loudly on the door.

"Préfect de Police!" He said loudly. "Open at once!"

"Moi Oui?" a maid asked, opening the door.

Seeing the target, a pretty 40 year old woman now at breakfast, lounging in her dressing gown, Priolet pushed the maid aside and walked up to the woman.

"Are you the woman Zelle, Marguerite known as Mata Hari?" he asked.

Margaretha casually finished her bite of food, blotted her lips with a cloth napkin then set it on the table before turning to look at the man.

"And what if I am?" she asked.

"Then, Having, both abroad and in France," he read out loud, "maintained intelligence with the agents of an enemy power for the purpose of furthering the undertakings of that power, and being answerable for the crime of having communicated to the latter numerous documents and information concerning the internal policy of France and the offensive of the spring of 1916, I place you under arrest."

He held forth the warrant and she took in in hand and looked it over before handing it back.

"Inspector," She said, looking him in the eye, "Mata Hari was just a stage name. One I haven't used in years."

"Regardless, you are one in the same person and this warrant for your arrest is signed by the Minister of War himself." He turned to the other officers. "I want a detailed search of this suite and her belongings! Now!"

"Do you have any objection to me putting some clothes on – or do you intend to force me out into this weather in my dressing gown?"

Giving her an annoyed look he gestured to her dressing screen. Stepping behind the screen, as she pulled her clothes on she listened to the officers rigorously turn her apartment upside down. Emerging dressed from behind the screen, she watched as they went about itemizing her visas and residence and travel permits, photographs, addresses, and correspondence, placing them all under seal.

Shaking her head, she pulled on a frock coat and buttoned it up.

Taking her by the arm, Priolet then escorted her out of the room, pausing for a moment at the door. "You men finish here," he said, "I will escort her to the Palace of Justice."

As Priolet led Margaretha through the hotel lobby, she shot the clerk behind the counter a quick look. He nodded slightly, and continued to watch as she was marched through the building and out the main doors.

The clerk then pulled a telephone from under the counter and quickly dialed a number.

"Hello? Monsieur Clunet? This is the clerk at the Élysées Palace Hotel. Madame McLeod would like you know the police are here..."

IT WAS JUST AFTER 11:00 o'clock that morning, Margaretha and Priolet entered the office of the Grand Inquisitor, 46 year-old Pierre Bouchardon, the Investigative Magistrate.

She was forcibly placed into the chair across from Bouchardon, who sat at his desk doing paperwork. He glanced up at Priolet and nodded. The inspector then turned and left the room, shutting the door behind him.

The room was silent as Bouchardon stood up, his eyes fixed on Margaretha, and stepped around his desk. Margaretha looked back at him and the two studied each other. He looked at her thick lips, dark skin, bits of dyed hair stinging out at her temples.

"You resemble a savage." He said with disgust.

"Disappointed are we?" she asked.

"Not in the least." He replied. "I am now satisfied I am in the presence of a person who was in the pay of our enemy - a born spy."

"Really... And just how did you come to that conclusion? I think they would have sought someone more - non-descript..."

"Because I *know* your kind!" he shouted, slamming his fist on the table. Margaretha didn't react – she just kept her eyes glued to his every move. "Feline, supple, artificial," Bouchardon continued, "used to gambling everything and anything without scruple - without pity, always ready to devour fortunes, leaving behind your ruined lovers to blow their brains out. In other words, you're a whore! Just like my wife – who'd left *me* to blow *my* brains out!"

Bouchardon finally finished and stood back. Margaretha gave him an annoyed look. "Whatever is wrong with you," She said, "is no little thing."

"Remember Robespierre's wise words," He stated, "Justice must know neither friend nor parents. She grinds in front of her all those who are guilty."

"What about those who are innocent?"

"Innocent or guilty," he said, spinning her chair around to look her in the face, *"You* I will grind into *dust!"*

"Priolet - come in here!"

"Sir." he said, stepping into the room.

"Send this whore to Saint-Lazare!" He looked Margaretha in the eye. "Now you will get a taste of what awaits you."

Just hearing the name of the infamous prison brought a haggard look into her eyes.

Bouchardon smiled with satisfaction as she was taken away.

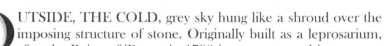

OUTSIDE, THE COLD, grey sky hung like a shroud over the imposing structure of stone. Originally built as a leprosarium, after the Reign of Terror in 1793 it was converted into an unheated women's prison. One hundred and twenty-three years later, although staffed by the Soeur de Marie-Joseph (Sisters of Mary and Joseph) Saint-Lazare had become a dank, dark, and foreboding place having housed such high profile prisoners as Henriette Caillaux and Marguerite Steinheil.

The footsteps of the women echoed off the red tile floor in the corridor, causing the rats to scurry between their feet. In the lead was Sister Léonide, the beads in the rosary at her side rattling with every step of the venerable mother superior. Following her walked 40 year-old, five foot five inch, Margaretha McLeod-Zelle, clutching her cloth frock coat tight around her, trying to ignore the scuttling vermin and gloomy atmosphere. On her heels and slightly to her left was a grim faced matron jailer, a large ring of keys in her hand. Following behind them was Sister Marie, one of those Sisters who personally attended the prisoners, supervising all the details of their monotonous lives.

When did it all go so wrong? She wondered as they trekked the dark, foreboding stone corridors. *How did M'Greet - the eldest child of four and Daddy's little darling - ever wind up here?*

January 1, 1883

THE SKY IN Leeuwarden, Netherlands, was sunny and bright and deceptively cold that New Year's morning as good looking Adam Zelle, in his silk top hat and flowered waist coat led his wife and family in a carriage to their newly purchased house on the Kelders.

As the excited six year-old Margaretha took in their new surroundings, her mother, Antje Zelle, had her hands full trying to comfort her fussy one-year olds, Ari and Cornelis, Margaretha's younger twin brothers.

"Where are we going, Papa Zelle?" Margaretha asked her father.

"To our new home at 28 Groote Kerkstraat, child. One of the best houses in town."

"And with our growing family," Antje added, "We're going to need the space."

"Relax, Antje." Adam told her. "Now that my investments have come in, if the home requires more servants we can easily afford them."

The carriage pulled to a stop in front of a lovely house – and there setting in the front yard stood a child-size four-seater carriage hitched to two beautifully horned goats.

"Papa Zelle!" Margaretha screamed in excitement. "Look!"

"It's all yours, my darling daughter." He said to Margaretha.

"Really Adam." Antje said as Margaretha ran over to the carriage and climbed into it. "Must you so openly indulged the girl? Just because you acted like a Baron when King William III visited the town a few years ago doesn't mean you are one."

"Maybe not, Antje, but my factory and the 3500 guilders I made from my oil investments are going to allow us to live like one."

"Don't you realize that putting on airs like this irks some of the citizens of Leeuwarden?"

"That is *their* problem..."

Antje just looked at her social climber husband, sighed, and shook her head.

"Madame McLeod!"

Hearing her name from Sister Léonide brought Margaretha back to the present.

"Yes ma'am?"

"Your number is 721-44625." Sister Léonide told Margaretha as they walked. "Remember it. And I am a *Sister* - of the order of Mary and Joseph – not a *ma'am*."

"Sorry."

"Look around." Sister Léonide suggested. Margaretha saw the austere and consoling figures wearing white Cornetts under their black veils which had a blue lining. Many also wore white aprons over their dark robes. "We Sisters have dedicated our entire lives in this place of penitence - to watch over our dear prisoners in order to give them a moral and religious education - as well as training in a trade."

Walking past one of the great dormitories, Margaretha witnessed a group prayer by the women within addressed to the image of the Virgin

12

on the wall decked out with faded artificial flowers. Following the example of the Sister, all the women stooped with more or less reverence before this symbol and uttered, with more or less sincerity, the prayer for a pure heart.

Margaretha took notice of how the eighty beds within, each neatly made up with their tight gray blankets and white bolsters, were arranged with perfect military symmetry in four rows across the tile floor.

With the prayer coming to a conclusion, the women exited the great dormitory in single file and proceeded down the corridor, passing them.

"Where are they going?" Margaretha asked.

"During the day, the prisoners are assembled in a workroom under the surveillance of a Sister, to whom it is confided the general oversight of the workrooms and the dormitories."

"Who stays in those?" Margaretha asked, gesturing to a double story of grated cells, each furnished with a bed, a stool, a shelf, and an earthenware vessel to use as a toilet.

"In le ménagerie?" Sister Léonide continued as they walked. "Only those who merit it by their good conduct. Now, according to the law, those merely accused of a crime and those actually convicted must be kept apart from each other. Thus, we've divided the prison into two sections. The first section is reserved for prisoners awaiting trial - and for convicts whose sentences are less than a year."

Sister Léonide came to a stop in front of a room sealed by a metal door. Upon the jailer opening the door, Margaretha took special notice of the mattresses standing on end, fastened to the walls.

"A padded cell?" She asked Sister Léonide.

"Just until we are sure you will not try and take your own life."

Margaretha entered the ten foot by ten foot room. The light coming in from the small window high on the wall was extremely dim illuminating the only furniture in the sparse cell, a bare mattress on the floor.

"Is there anything you want?" Sister Léonide asked her.

"Yes." Margaretha replied. "A telephone and a bath."

13

"Since you have been charged with espionage," The Sister told her, "Captain Bouchardon has ordered that for the first 24 hours you be under constant supervision. It is for your own good."

"No," Margaretha replied, "It is so that I do not deprive him of the pleasure of seeing me shot by committing suicide first."

The iron door closed against its frame with a loud clang and she listened as the key turned the lock. Sitting on the bed, she looked up at the small window and the fleeting daylight.

So, now I am just another number in Saint Lazare - a prison for streetwalkers with venereal disease. A far cry from Miss Buys' school on the Hofplein.

1888

MISS BUYS, A tiny, unmarried woman with a slight limp, walked the aisles of her school room with a wooded ruler in hand, ready to rap the knuckles of any insolent schoolgirl who insisted upon displaying bad manners.

Seeing ten year-old Margaretha laughing and giggling with her friend, Ybeltje, Miss Buys walked up behind the girls and wacked the desk with her ruler. The two girls immediately straightened up.

"Miss Zelle – do you really consider that ladylike behavior?"

Margaretha, suppressing a smile, shook her head.

Miss Buys looked at the slender girl with long black hair and daringly flamboyant red and yellow dress.

"Don't you know a young lady simply doesn't wear such a dress to school?"

Margaretha shrugged.

"Then why do you wear it?"

"Just to be different."

"Miss Buys," Ybeltje said, "M'greet[1] just likes to shine."

"And her dressing this way doesn't make you jealous?"

Ybeltje shook her head. "No ma'am."

---

[1] Pronounced M'great

MARGARETHA SPENT THE first night in prison alone, sitting with her feet up on the mattress, listening to the rats scurry around her and wondering how they managed to get in and out of the secured cell. The night seemed endless.

The absence of bathing facilities was maddening – especially for a woman who considered cleanliness a great virtue. Shortly after the grey dawn, she heard a key rattle in the door's lock and watched as it opened and Sister Léonide entered.

"From our observation over the last fourteen hours I believe it is safe to conclude that you will remain on your good behavior, is it not?"

"Yes Sister."

"Then come with me."

Margaretha gathered her few things together and climbed off her bed. "Gladly." She said, departing the grim dank cell.

As they walked to her new accommodations, there came a commotion as two large men forcibly hauled a kicking and screaming woman down the corridor. Margaretha could only watch as the terrified, seemingly mad woman fought against the men with every effort in her body as they dragged her away.

Margaretha gave Sister Léonide a questioning glance.

"They are taking her to a solitary confinement cell." The sister explained. "We warned her to stop her disruptive behavior. The cells are tiny, poorly lit, stifling in summer and freezing in winter with only a naked plank for a bed."

"Who are those men?" Margaretha asked.

"There are a handful of male guardians who are reserved for this sort of work and tend to the overall security of the prison. They are available if there is a discipline problem that we sisters cannot handle." Sister Léonide explained. "They can only enter the prison interior with authorization prison's director."

A short walk with the sister and jailer led them to an iron barred cell, larger than the others, above which was painted the number '12.' Sister Léonide turned and faced Margaretha as the matron selected one of the keys on her ring, unlocked and opened the door.

Stepping inside a room twice as large as the padded cell, Margaretha looked over the three beds. From the few personal items visible, two were already occupied by other women. She turned to Sister Léonide.

"Welcome to de la pistole." Sister Léonide explained.

"I don't understand."

"Cells #12, #13, #14 are reserved - rented at seven and a half Francs per month - paid in advance, of course."

"Of course." Margaretha paused. "Wait – paid for by whom?"

"In your case, I believe it is the French government."

"Really?"

"La pistole is reserved for elite prisoners, typically two or three to a cell, who are awaiting trial for a first offense that is not a morals charge. You have been pre-approved by the prison director to enjoy this privilege."

"Privilege?"

"Yes. You are largely exempt from following the regular prison routine."

Margaretha raised her eyebrows.

"You will be attended to by a staff of four maids. And, if you so desire and can pay for it, we can arrange for your meals to be catered."

"Now that I am no longer renting a hotel room, I can pay for it."

"Inside." The matron ordered.

Margaretha stepped inside, the iron bars sliding closed and locking behind her. A rat, startled by the noise, scurried across the floor as she sat down on the bed with a bare mattress, and looked around.

Then Sister Marie entered with two folded sheets and a blanket, handing them to her.

"Your meal." Sister Marie said, sliding in a tray with a bowl and spoon on it.

"What is it?"

"Because you are in here, consommé and coffee for breakfast. You will receive a plate of meat and vegetables and coffee for lunch – soup and a meat course for dinner."

16

Margaretha looked over the meager meal. "Not exactly what they serve at the Hôtel Élysée. What would I get if I was in the regular population?"

"Soup and bread – with a piece of meat on Sunday." The Sister was quiet for a moment. "Is it true," Sister Marie asked, "That you are the famous Mata Hari?"

Margaretha sighed, taking her tray "I may not resemble a supple dancer in this pallid light – but yes," she said, "It is true." She sighed. "But now - that seems like a lifetime ago."

"All rise at five o'clock in summer and at six, or half-past six, the rest of the year. Now that you are in number twelve, permission has been given for you to take a fifteen minute walk each day in the prison courtyard. All lights out at eight."

Margaretha nodded and glanced at the two made beds.

"Who are they?" She asked.

"Other women inmates awaiting trial. They perform cleaning and other light jobs during the day." Sister Marie explained. You'll meet them when they return sometime after 5:00 o'clock this evening. Meanwhile, either Reverend Jules Arboux or Father Dommergue, whichever is your choice, will visit you."

Margaretha shrugged. "Tell them not to bother. I have no particular religious belief."

Sister Marie turned to leave – then caught herself. "Oh – and I have been informed one Edouard Clunet will be visiting you later today."

"Good. He's my solicitor."

Edouard Clunet came to her cell in the mid-afternoon. However, with the gloomy dark grey skies overhead, the time of day seemed not to change.

Margaretha sat on the edge of her now made bed as the 74 year-old man paced the cell, telling her the situation.

"According to military law, I am only allowed to be present during your first and last interrogation." He explained. "And I am assured that Monsieur Bouchardon sticks to the very letter of the law."

"Can you do anything about the dreadful conditions in here?"

"Believe it or not, being in cell number twelve, you are already receiving the best treatment this prison can offer."

"At least when my friends come to see me it will offer me some comfort."

Clunet looked at her, then sat down on the bed next to her.

"Margaretha," He told her, "the moment you walked in here, your friends deserted you like rats fleeing a sinking ship."

"Why?" She asked, the light leaving her eyes. "Whatever do you mean?"

"You must remember – there is a war on and you have been arrested for espionage. They are afraid of ruining their reputations – or of possibly being arrested themselves."

"When I was detained in London, I wrote to the Netherlands Legation. I will do that again as soon as you leave."

"Good. Include everything that has happened. And when Bouchardon asks you some pre-trial questions, which I'm sure he will do, just tell him the truth."

"I have been." She said dejectedly. "And look where it's got me."

Chapter 2

"Amidst a thousand dandelions
One shining orchid stands."

❖   ❖   ❖

March 3, 1917

A SOMEWHAT SURPRISED, Reverend Jules Arboux, accompanied by the jailer, appeared at her cell to find Margaretha sitting alone, reading, as usual, her cell mates off doing their chores.

The door was unlocked and the bars slid aside.

"Margaretha," He said, "you can imagine how surprised I was to get your message – especially since you've refused to see me every time I come down here."

"Yes, reverend. I was wondering if you would accompany me on my walk this morning."

He smiled and nodded his approval.

A few minutes later found the reverend and Margaretha walking the circuit, a circular route just inside the prison walls that allowed, for fifteen minutes a day at least, the female prisoners to talk freely amongst themselves.

19

A chill from the winter air not yet departed the early spring air and caused Margaretha to clutch her coat tight around her. Arboux, wearing his black hat and long cassock, walked beside her, his hands clasped behind his back. Both strolled in silence at first.

"I suppose you're wondering why my dark hair and olive complexion is so different than that of most other Dutch women..." She stated.

"My concern is that of a person's soul – not the color of their skin."

"I am descended from the Woudkers – on my mother's branch of the van der Meulen family."

"That dark complexioned tribe that once lived in the forests of Friesland?"

Margaretha nodded.

"Interesting."

"The truth is, I've always desired to be different. When I was eleven, my friend Ybeltje wrote a poem about me: Amidst a thousand dandelions - One shining orchid stands."

"You know what the Bible says about vanity."

"I know – but I can't help it. As a little girl I loved to find myself the focal point of my friends' admiration. I still do. Is that so wrong?"

"Margaretha, there are others even here in this facility that view your past behavior as impudence." Arboux told her. "I, however, suspect it is simply part and parcel of your nature."

The two walked on in silence for a few minutes.

"I have never told this to anyone before," She said with a faraway look, "but my childhood came to an end on the night of July 15, 1889 - just three weeks before my thirteenth birthday."

The reverend paused his walking and gently took her by the shoulder, looking her in the eye.

"What are you saying, my child?"

"You have to understand - once again Papa invested money from his hat factory in an oil drilling scheme. Only this time he was defrauded. It bankrupted his company, leaving dozens of hard-working people without a job. He went from the Baron of Leeuwarden to pariah overnight."

"I still don't..."

"Mama wasn't there when he came home that afternoon." Tears started welling up in her eyes. "He told me a good daughter would comfort her father..."

Horror filled Reverend Arboux's eyes and he swallowed hard, realizing what he was about to hear.

Antje, a box of groceries in her hands, entered the house, setting them on the kitchen table. As she began to unpack them she paused when a noise, like two people rustling about, from another part of the house got her attention.

Stepping up to the cracked open bedroom door, she pushed it all the way open – her eyes widening with the shock of what she saw. Screaming, she turned and ran to the back door, where she leaned out and threw up.

Adam, pulling up and belting his trousers, appeared at her side.

"Antje," he started. "Let me..."

"GET OUT!" She shouted without looking at him. "Get out of my house THIS INSTANT!! YOU PIG!!"

Adam turned away and gathering only a few personal things, left the house like an animal with its tail between its legs - as Antje collapsed on the back steps, sobbing.

"What did your mother say to you?"

"Nothing. When I tried to explain, she cut me short saying she didn't want to hear it. We never spoke of it again."

Margaretha continued on her walk. The reverend said a prayer as he shook his head and watched her walk away.

April 16, 1917

SISTER LÉONIDE WALKED up to cell number twelve with the matron jailer in tow. Margaretha, sitting on her bed, hearing them approach, lowered her book and glanced at them.

"It is a beautiful sunny day outside." Sister Léonide told her as the matron unlocked the door. "You will enjoy your walk today."

Margaretha walked onto the prison courtyard and looked around at the other groups of women prisoners gathered about the yard in small groups, walking and talking amongst themselves and enjoying the sunshine.

The 41 year-old tried to ignore the oppressive high stone walls enclosing the grounds, glancing up at and concentrating on the bright blue sky overhead – and sighed.

"Is the weather not to your liking?" Sister Léonide asked.

"No – you were absolutely correct in saying this is a beautiful day..."

"Then what troubles you?"

"I just don't understand why I haven't heard back from the Dutch Legation..."

"I should not tell you this," Sister Léonide said calmly, "but it is because your letters have never left the prison."

Margaretha turned abruptly, ready to confront the sister.

"Please!" Sister Léonide said, raising her open palms. "Allow me to explain. It was Monsieur Bouchardon's orders."

"I am listening."

"I do not approve of his methods," The Sister told her, "But have no say I the matter – I just follow orders." She stepped closer to Margaretha and lowered her voice. "I overheard him talking on the telephone the other night, saying that your arrest has been kept secret these last two months in hopes that the Germans would communicate about you to their office in Madrid."

"Well?"

"Nothing. And he is beside himself."

Margaretha looked around at the other women prisoners – no one was paying her any attention.

"If I wrote *another* letter to the Dutch Legation," Margaretha asked, "would *you* make sure they received it?"

Sister Léonide was silent for a few moments as she contemplated the proposal. She then nodded slightly.

"I will give it to my friend in the French Foreign office."

So as not to draw any attention to themselves, they then continued the walk around the courtyard.

April 22, 1917

A SECRETARY AT the Dutch Legation in Paris was at her desk, going through the day's paperwork when she was handed a letter by an office boy.

"From the Quai d'Orsay." He said, handing it to her.

"What is the French Foreign office sending us?" She asked, taking the envelope in hand.

The boy just shrugged and continued on his rounds.

Opening the letter, she glanced over the contents:

"Semi-officially we have been informed that Margretha McLeod-Zelle is imprisoned at Saint Lazare. She is suspected of espionage. The authorities investigate the case, which seems to be very serious."

The woman was momentarily stunned, the jumped to her feet.

"I need to send a telegram to The Hague!" she shouted. "Now!"

REVEREND ARBOUX PAUSED before Margaretha's cell later that day. Instead of ignoring him or sending him away as she had a number of times in the past, she gestured that he come in and talk with her.

"I've been waiting for you to return." Margaretha said to him as he entered the cell. "I have a feeling I know what you want to talk about."

"If you're referring to the incident with your father – you are mistaken. It is none of my business."

"Then what do you want?"

"I've heard all kinds of wild stories about you. One of them says you're actually a Malaysian princess..."

Margaretha smiled. "That is one of my favorites."

"But it's not true."

"No. It is one of the tales I made up about Mata Hari."

"The name you call yourself when dancing..."

She nodded.

"What actually happened after your father left?"

23

Margaretha sat with her back against the wall and collected her thoughts.

"Well, me, Momma and my three brothers were forced to leave the house at 28 Groote Kerkstraat and move to a modest upstairs apartment on the Willemskade F30." She was thoughtful for a moment. "It wasn't long after the move I first noticed Momma was sick and physically she began to deteriorate."

"Do you know what was wrong with her?"

Margaretha nodded. "She had the TB. She died at age 49, less than two years later. Just a couple of months before my fifteenth birthday."

On the afternoon of the funeral, Margaretha's friend, Ybeltje, was passing the apartment when she heard someone playing a haunting tune on the piano inside.

Ybeltje stepped to the window and glanced inside to see 15 year-old Margaretha, tears streaming down her face, at the keyboard. Ybeltje let herself inside and watched Margaretha quietly until she finished.

"I didn't know you could play like that." Ybeltje said to her.

"It was the *pain* I felt!" Margaretha told her in a trembling voice, emotion clouding her eyes.

"What about your father?" The reverend asked.

"Him? He had moved to Amsterdam to be with another woman a year earlier. I'll never forget her name - Susanna Catharina ten Hoove."

"Why is that?"

Margaretha laughed. "The witch couldn't stand me! Or my younger brother, Johannes, for that matter. She sent *him* to Franeker to be with Momma's relatives."

Arboux was about to continue with his questioning when Sister Léonide appeared at the bars of cell number twelve with the matron jailer.

"I'm sorry, Reverend." The sister said as the matron unlocked the cell. "But Monsieur Bouchardon wishes to speak with madame."

Margaretha glanced at the reverend and rolled her eyes.

"Again?" She asked Sister Léonide. "He has already interviewed me six times. I really have nothing new to tell him."

24

The reverend stood as she did.

"Perhaps we can continue our conversation later?" He asked.

Margaretha smiled and nodded and was then led away by Sister Léonide.

❖   ❖   ❖

Chapter 3

"I wanted to live like a butterfly in the sun."

ONCE AGAIN Margaretha was marched into office of forty-six year-old Captain Pierre Bouchardon. She sighed as she took her chair. She tried not to look at him - his thin moustache, high forehead and arched eyebrows – as he questioned her. Once again she quickly grew tired of his voice, his inane questioning, her every word being weighed and examined by him in minute detail.

How had her life come to this? She couldn't help but wonder if things would have turned out different if her father's new wife, Susanna, hadn't treated her with such distain...

November 1891

Fifteen year-old Margaretha stood next the open door of the living room in her father's house, listening to Adam and Susanna arguing.

"I will gladly accept Ari and Cornelis, into our home." Susanna told Adam, giving him an ultimatum. "But if *you* are ever to have *me* for your wife, Margaretha *must* go!"

"But – she's my daughter!"

"Why?! All she has to do is snap her fingers and she gets anything she wants!"

"But..."

"And those dark gloating eyes of hers..." Susanna said, imitating a wide eyed stare, "I can feel them taunting me!" she let out a shudder. "No, Adam – either *she* goes – or *I* go – that is all there is to it."

Adam let out a frustrated sigh. "All right." He said. "I'll get ahold of her godfather in Sneek." He contemplated for a moment. "And I know you're having problems with young Johannes, also. I believe his mother's family in Franeker will take him."

Susanna, her arms folded across her chest, just stood looking at him. "We'll see." She said. "We'll see."[2]

Little did anyone realize that with the family unit completely dismantled Margaretha would never see or contact her brothers again.

March 1893

FOR THE NEXT year, 16 year-old Margaretha attended school in Sneek, her godfather, one Mr. Visser, noticing that as she matured, the more the teenage boys started noticing his openly flirtatious goddaughter. Attempting to stall any result of the male-female union he saw as inevitable, he remembered his friend, 51-year-old Wybrandus Haanstra, the Headmaster of a boarding school in Leiden.

Telling Margaretha it was time she thought about her future and about how she was going to make a living, Mr. Visser convinced her that she should train to become a kindergarten teacher. Although she was definitely not fit for such a career, Margaretha, bowing to his wishes, enrolled in the boarding school and began her teacher training.

Headmaster Wybrandus was an industrious attractive middle-aged man who had long since settled into a comfortable but cool relationship

---

[2] Adam Zelle finally married Susanna Catharina ten Hoove in Amsterdam on February 9, 1893.

with his wife. His attention focused on the running of the school, at first he was indifferent to Margaretha, just as he was to all the new students.

Then, one day in March of 1893, he rounded the corner of a busy hallway in the school, accidentally running into Margaretha, and knocking her books and papers to the floor.

"Pardon me." He said, bending over and gathering the books and papers in his hands.

Standing, he came face to face with the dark, attractive, five foot ten inch Margaretha – and froze – feeling a stirring inside.

"I... I..." He said, handing her the books.

"Thank you." Margaretha said with a coy smile.

All he could do was watch her swaying hips as she walked away.

"Why Mr. Wybrandus!" an older matron teacher said, walking up to him. "Control yourself! You're acting like a love-sick schoolboy!"

He quickly collected himself and embarrassed over his actions, made his way into his office. Shutting the door, he leaned against it, panting. He then noticed his palms were sweating and wiped them off on the legs of his trousers.

"Oh my god." He said to himself, his heart pounding. "That girl! She makes my blood boil!"

January 1894

THE SAME MATRON teacher that noticed his behavior in the school hallway, marched up to the door of Margaretha's dormitory room and rapped on the door.

"Miss Zelle?!" She said anxiously. "I've been informed there's a boy in your room! That better not be true! You know the rules! I'm coming in!"

Throwing the door open, to her shock and dismay, she found Margaretha having sex – with the headmaster.

"Mr. Wybrandus!" The matron cried, "This is most unacceptable!"

"It's not my fault!" He said, climbing off the girl, and nervously gathering his clothes up off the floor. "She... She enticed me! I couldn't help myself!"

The matron just looked at him and frowned.

"I want her expelled – immediately! Contact Mr. Visser and have him pick her up." Wybrandus ordered as he pulled on his clothes. "If she can do this to me – just think of what she could do to the young men in the area."

Margaretha, sitting up and covering herself with the sheet, looked at him in disbelief.

June 1894

FRAMED BY THE window of the passenger car she rode in, Margaretha, dressed in her best clothes and a carpet bag beside her on the seat, sat by herself in the otherwise empty car. The steam whistle sounded and the locomotive left a cloud of smoke in the air as it chugged southward towards The Hague in the middle of the night.

Stepping onto the platform of the train station in The Hague the next morning, Margaretha found her Aunt Geertruida waiting for her.

"I am so glad you agreed to take me in."

"I heard what happened at the school, dear." Aunt Geertruida said, comforting Margaretha. "And having delt with men like him my entire life, know how these things come about."

"Mr. Visser said my behavior brought shame on his family." Margaretha explained. "It took me three months to save up enough for train fare."

As they walked from the platform, Margaretha noticed the number of men in uniform walking about.

"I do so love men in uniform." Margaretha said casually.

"You'll see plenty of them here." Aunt Geertruida told her. "Lots of officers from the Colonial Army in the Dutch East Indies spend their leave in The Hague."

"They do? Why?"

"Because we're the closest city to the beach resort at Scheveningen."

"I do believe I'm going to love my stay in The Hague."

29

August 1894

Now home in Amsterdam, 38 year-old Captain Rudolf Johnathan McLeod[3] found himself most evenings sitting outdoors at the Café American on the Leidseplein overlooking the canal. Five foot ten, sturdily built and nearly completely bald, he wore a long sweeping moustache.

As usual, this day he sat drinking when only real friend, journalist for the Amsterdam *News of the Day*, J. T. Z. de Balbian Verster, approached.

"John – its so good to see you." Balbian said, shaking his hand then sitting down. "You've only been serving in the Indies for what? Twenty years now?"

"Seventeen. Since I was promoted to second lieutenant in 1877." He let out a sigh. "Believe me, I've had to deal with tough specimens of the human race."

"I can tell. The experience has hardened you."

"You said you're back home for - how long?"

"Two years."

"With the Atjeh War still going strong? But you're in the Colonial Army - how did you manage that?"

"Well, during the past ten years we've been fighting I've come down with malaria, cholera, diabetes, typhus, tropical parasites, syphilis, and even diabetes. Left me with lingering rheumatism of the joints."

Balbian shook his head in disbelief.

"Last June my physical condition got so serious that I had to be carried aboard the *SS Prinses Marie* on a stretcher."

"You staying with your sister, Louise – I mean Tante Lavies?"

John nodded.

Balbian leaned close to John. "Tell me - why does a 36 year-old woman insist on being called *Aunt* Louise?"

---

[3] Often seen spelled MacLeod, Margaretha spelled it McLeod so I will also.

John shrugged. "I don't know. It all started right after her husband died."

"Well, it was good seeing you." Balbian said, getting up to leave. "Let's do this again."

"Any time. Louise lives right around the corner. I'll most likely be here just about every evening."

March 2, 1895

MARGARETHA, NOW A strikingly good looking eighteen year-old, was still living with her aunt in The Hague. Out of school with nothing much to do in the cool March weather, the young romantic woman spent each evening pouring over the lonely hearts section of *The News of the Day*.

Coming to one of the personal ads she paused and read it aloud.

"Officer on home leave from Dutch East Indies would like to meet girl of pleasant character. Object – matrimony."

The ad set her thinking. In her mind she envisioned an elaborate marriage to a young soldier in a crisp uniform brimming with medals and gold braid. She pictured herself moving back into the Dutch upper class and reattaining the standard of living she had so enjoyed growing up.

Returning to reality, Margaretha immediately penned John a letter, enclosing a photograph of herself, and addressing it to *The News of the Day* in Amsterdam.

HAVING BECOME AN almost nightly ritual, Captain McLeod and Balbian once again sat drinking at "their table" at the café at dusk while looking out over the canal.

"You know," Captain McLeod lamented, "these past few months I've been giving serious thought to settling down."

31

"So you've been telling me for the past two months. What's the problem?"

"I'm worried about attracting a "decent" woman."

"What do you mean by that?'

"Louise says I've spent so long away from civilization - that I've forgotten the finer points of the social graces."

"Such as..."

"She says my language is army-course and unrefined, and that I am often too loud in mixed company."

"Forget Louise – how do you see yourself?"

"As an outspoken, hard-bitten, tough, but thoroughly straightforward soldier, with a heart of gold."

"You know John, you're constant complaining about this - but I've never seen you *do* anything about it. If you're really *that* desperate, why don't you just place an ad in the lonely hearts section of my newspaper, *The News of the Day?*"

"No," he said, waving the idea off, "I wouldn't even know what to say..."

"I figured you'd say something like that." Balbian said, producing a copy of the newspaper. "That's why I wrote an ad up and placed in the paper myself."

"What?" John said, opening up the paper. "No! You didn't!"

"Oh yes I did – It's been running for the last two weeks - read it."

"I ought to..." John leveled his gaze at Balbian. "You've wasted your time and efforts because if I receive any letters, I'm sure as hell not going to open them!"

"You mean – letters like this?" Balbian said, pulling a half-dozen envelopes from his jacket pocket. John took them in hand and looked at them in wide eyed amazement. "The newspaper started receiving those before the end of the first week." Balbian explained.

John then regained his stern composure, tucking the envelopes into his coat pocket.

"Aren't you going to open any of them?" Balbian asked.

"Later - if I get around to it."

Balbian looked at him and sighed.

32

Later that night, alone in his room at his sister's mansion, John, now fascinated, smiled. Pulling out the envelopes, he began opening and reading the letters with genuine interest.

The first couple of letters resulted in only a raised eyebrow, one being from a widow with five children, the other being from a sixty-three year-old spinster.

Then he picked up an envelope and marveled at the exquisite handwriting. Unfolding the letter inside, a photograph dropped out. Picking it up, John was momentarily stunned by beautiful young girl in the picture. Upon reading Margaretha's letter, he was, to say the least, intrigued. Pulling out a sheet of paper and dipping his pen into a bottle of ink, he eagerly responded to her letter.

March 20, 1895

THAT AFTERNOON, while John and Balbian shared drinks at the Café American, Balbian broached the subject of the ad.

"Say John, did you ever read any of those letters?"

"Actually," John said, embarrassed, "I've been trading letters for a couple of weeks with one of the females who answered the ad."

"What? Really?"

John took out Margaretha's photograph and showed it to him. "I didn't mean to keep the correspondence a secret from you – but her name's Margaretha Zelle – and she seems to be quite a girl."

"If this is really a picture of her - I'll say."

"I need your advice."

"Shoot."

"Well, in her last letter, Margaretha proposed we meet somewhere face to face. I've already had to postpone one meeting after I suffered a severe attack of rheumatism."

"How about the Rijksmuseum here in Amsterdam?"

"I like it." John said, thinking it over. "I'll write to Margaretha today and set up the meet."

March 24, 1895

It was a drizzly cold Sunday afternoon when Margaretha and John met for the first time at the Rijksmuseum. John was immediately stricken with the charming, dark eyed, black haired young woman that looked several years older than her age.

"Rudolf McLeod?" She asked, walking up to him and offering her hand. "I'm Margaretha Zelle."

"Seeing this handsome young man made my heart start to beat faster.... I wanted to live like a butterfly in the sun – rather than bored and comfortable in the claustrophobic calmness of the inside of my room."

"Pleased to meet you." He said, kissing her hand. "But please, Griet[4], call me by my middle name, John."

To both the attraction was immediate. Six days later, March 30, they were engaged. Soon afterwards, John again came down with a crippling attack of rheumatism. This one was so serious he was unable to even write to her, finally asking his sister Louise to do so for him.

Margaretha continued to stay with her aunt in The Hague for the next few months, making frequent trips to Amsterdam to see John.

"My dearest Johnie," she wrote in reply to one of his letters one Wednesday evening, "Oh, darling, I feel such pity for you, and I am so terribly sorry that our plan once again has gone wrong. All accidents happen at once, don't they? Well, John, don't feel too bad about it, *tootie*. When I come to see you on Sunday I hope the pain will be gone.

"Did you suffer much, and couldn't you write me yourself? I guess not, could you? For otherwise you would have done so.

"Do you think you'll be able to walk again on Sunday? I do hope so, darling, but try not to overdo it. Yes, it made me feel very sad at first, but I considered it from the gay and sensible point of view. For, if I just sit here and feel dismal, that won't help you a bit, will it?

---

[4] Pronounced Greet

34

"Louise wrote me: 'I hope for both of you that in a few weeks at the city hall everything will be floating on sunshine.'

"Well, I hope so, too. And you, John? What do you think? You'd better be brave and gay, for that brings the best results. Your little wife always does that, and if I had not, my gaiety would have worn off a long time ago. Do you expect me Sunday?

"When you are able to, will you write me and let me know how you are feeling? Just give me a wonderful kiss, and just imagine that I am with you – that's what I do too.

"Well, Johnie, adieu with a delicious kiss from your so very loving wife, Greta."

July 10, 1895

I DON'T KNOW exactly how to tell you this," John said to Margaretha as they sat at the Café American that summer evening, "But *no one* in my strict military family can get married without the official sanction of my uncle Norman..."

Margaretha gave him a quizzical look. "But that's positively barbaric." She told him. "This is not the seventeenth century..."

"I know – I know. But he's a retired General and head of the family – and I'm not one to buck family tradition. That's why I'd like you to meet him..."

"You worried I won't pass inspection?"

"Not at all."

Margaretha sighed, leaning back in her chair and folding her arms.

"Please," John said, "for me?"

"All right. When?"

"Sunday afternoon – right after church."

"I don't go to church..."

"I know – but Uncle Norman does."

While not a mansion, Uncle Norman's house was of substantial size with two stories amid an expanse of a well-kept green lawn in front and an exquisite garden in the back. And that's just wat Margaretha could see from their carriage as it pulled up the red brick drive leading to the house.

A few minutes later she stood in what appeared to her to be an immense library, with books on shelves from floor almost to the ten foot ceiling. In full military uniform, his hands clasped behind his back, Uncle Norman silently strolled his living room looking over Margaretha, mumbling under his breath. For a few moments the situation was tense.

"Young – but good looking." He said repeatedly. "Damn good looking!"

John gave his uncle and expectant look – and the General nodded slightly. Relieved, John smiled. Margaretha let out pensive sigh, realizing she had passed the inspection.

Once outside the General's fine home and back in their carriage, Margaretha turned to John.

"Johnnie, I know I told you I was an orphan," she said, "but I have a confession to make – I have a father."

John thought about it for a moment then shrugged. "That happens in the best of families."

"You don't understand – because I am underage I need his permission to marry. But before he'll sign anything he's demanded that we come and visit him."

"Where does he live?"

"At 148 on the Lange Leidschedwarsstraat."

"Okay – but that's a pretty decrepit part of Amsterdam."

"I know. That's probably why when I told him you are an officer from an excellent family he demanded that we come and see him in a large carriage instead of a simple one horse cab."

"Why?"

"Knowing my father, I suspect he hopes the horses and carriage in the poor neighborhood where he lives will cause a sensation."

John took a deep breath, resolving himself. "Just remember - I'm marrying *you* – *not* your whole family. Let's go and get his consent."

Upon meeting John and seeing that he was an older military man and not some young kid, Adam consented to the marriage. Margaretha asked him to be at city hall the next day, where his presence was required to sign the appropriate documents.

On July 11, 1895, just three and a half months after they met, and three and a half weeks before her 19th birthday, John and Margaretha prepared to get married in the city hall of Amsterdam.

As John and his sister, Louise approached the building, she became pensive and anxious.

"Johnny," she said, taking him aside, "I beg of you - don't do it!"

He just looked at her.

"Stop it, Louise." He told her. "I know that you think Margaretha is little more than a mutt without a pedigree - but I refuse to allow you to keep us apart."

"Johnnie! Can't you see I'm trying to keep you from making a fatal mistake?!"

"And Can't you see I'm tired of being alone?" he replied, pulling his arm free from her grasp. "Up until now I have called the army

home - but believe me, sister, when I tell you they're not much to snuggle up with at night."

The ceremony at city hall was a quiet affair – completely the opposite of the boisterous celebration afterwards. All of Adam Zelle's friends and neighbors thronged the pavement along the canal, wildly cheering the newlyweds proceeding to the Café American for their wedding lunch. A luncheon which Adam failed attend because John had deliberately given Adam's cab driver instructions that took him to the other side of town.

Chapter 4

"Oh how I longed to drift away from them."

❖   ❖   ❖

THEIR HONEYMOON was a modest affair, in Wiesbaden, Germany. John quickly discovered to his chagrin that Margaretha, because of the regal way she carried herself, turned the heads of arrogant young officers as if "they could spin completely around." Few of the military men refrained from making overt advances to, and loud remarks about, his young Dutch bride when John finally confronted the young men.

"Gentlemen," he said, "that is no lady – that is *my* wife!"

And he walked off, arm in arm with Margaretha.

At their hotel later, John, his wallet in hand, checked over his finances then turned to Margaretha, who sat at her dressing table, combing her hair.

"Our honeymoon is going to have to be cut short." He told her.

"Why?" She asked innocently.

"Because my sick pay is far from sufficient to sustain this mode of life. The expense of the wedding and honeymoon have just about drained me of my ready cash."

"So what are we going to do when we get back to Amsterdam?"

"There is only one thing we can do - accept my sister's invitation for you and I to live with her at 79 Leidschekade."

"Convenient for you - since it's practically around the corner from the Café American." She said, turning to look at him. "But, John, that domineering battleax hates me! I've felt it from the first moment I met her."

John suddenly slapped Margaretha across the mouth, almost knocking her off the dressing table chair.

"Shut up, bitch!" He shouted. "That's my sister you're talking about!" He stepped away, collecting himself as Margaretha checked in the dressing table mirror to see if he had bruised her. "She's a widow, living all alone in that big house - and I, for one, am not going to pass up this opportunity."

Margaretha, looking at him in the mirror, frowned.

"Mrs. Mueller at the hairdresser was right about you!" Margaretha shouted at John. "You're a crude brute! She warned me you being married wouldn't limit the attraction you felt for other women! Your eyes are always roving!"

"So what?! I'm married – not dead! Now hurry up. I don't want to be late for that Hotel and Travel Sector exposition."

Margaretha sighed. "I still don't understand why you want to go to that. It's not like we own a hotel..."

"Because N.A. Calisch is supposed to be there."

"Who?!"

"He's the chairman of the exposition's executive committee."

"So? I still don't..."

"Just shut up you dumb bitch – and make yourself decent."

John, decked out in a clean crisp uniform, and Margaretha in her finest, appeared at the exposition in style. Stepping from their carriage into the bustling ornamental gardens in front of the hotel, she immediately turned the heads of all the men, even those with a woman already on their arms.

N.A. Calisch, standing with a male friend near the entrance of the hotel, noticed the couple

40

"I just don't understand it." Calisch said to his friend, watching Margaretha and her husband. "What does a lively, young and attractive girl like that see in an old soldier like McLeod?"

The man glanced at the couple and shook his head. "I wish I knew." He said. "Then she'd be on my arm and not his."

Calisch shook his head.

Later that evening, Calisch sat at a writing desk in his hotel room going over some papers when a knock came at his door. Glancing at a clock on the wall he saw it was nearly 10:30 p.m. Opening the door he was greeted by John in uniform, hat in hand.

"Captain McLeod." Calisch said in greeting. "I thought everyone had gone home by now. What can I do for you at this hour?"

"May I come in? It is a personal matter and I'd like to talk to you..."

Calisch, cautious, but curious, lingered at the door for a moment before finally opening it wide and stepping aside to let John enter.

"First of all," John said, walking into the room, "I want to thank you for going out of your way to make sure my wife and I have had a good time. I must say, I was especially impressed with the life size model of the *Prinz Hendrick*."

"A fine ship. Now, what I can I do for the officer of the Queen's army?"

"Did you know that I am the son of Captain John Brienen McLeod, a descendant of the Gesto branch of the McLeod's of Skye?"

"So that's where you get the Scottish surname."

John nodded. "And that my sister is Dina Louisa, the Baroness Sweerts de Landas?"

"No, I did not know that." Calisch said, now suspecting John had come for a purpose and not to simply exchange pleasantries. "Captain McLeod – it is getting late. What is this about?"

"Mr. Calisch, at present I am home in the middle of a two year sick leave and am trying to support my wife and I on my meager sick pay."

41

Calisch sat on the corner of his desk, his arms folded across his chest, studying the man. "Go on." He said, resting his chin in his left hand.

"It is with great reluctance," John continued, "that I am asking to barrow three thousand guilders."

"That is a sizeable sum of money."

"I realize that sir. And in a year or so I will be retiring from the army on a full thirty year pension – but *then* doesn't help me *now*."

"And just *how* would you pay this back?"

"With the first payment from my pension you will be repaid in full."

"You seem to be an honorable man, McLeod." Calisch said, standing and pacing the floor, thinking. "Your sister *is* a Baroness... and it appears once you retire, you will be a man of some resources. Is that correct?"

John nodded.

Calisch sat down at his desk, opened his checkbook and began filling out a check for three thousand guilders.

"And just what did he do with that money?" Bouchardon asked.

Margaretha shrugged. "What did not go to pay off some old debts, was quickly consumed."

"Consumed? Could you enlighten us?"

"John continued to drink and carouse at the Café American as if he were still a carefree bachelor." Margaretha lamented. "But the money ran out quickly and his debts began mounting again - growing like piles of winter snow."

"And just when did Captain McLeod repay this loan?"

"He never did."

"Why not? He retired with a full thirty year pension, did he not?'

"Yes. But his annual pension was far less than the one time loan."

"Didn't Mr. Calisch ever seek to collect it?"

"He did." Margaretha said, somewhat ashamed. "But John always seemed to know when he was coming and made sure *not* to be there.

In fact, he gave me special instructions on what to do when Mr. Calisch appeared."

"And just what were those 'special instructions?'"

"I was told to 'be nice to him' as a form of repayment."

"Meaning what, exactly?"

"I was to have sex with him."

"Did you?"

"No! When I told Mr. Calisch what John said, the man became incensed and disgusted - then left."

"Is that all that happened?"

"With me, yes. But John was often gone from the house during the evening..."

Just after sunset, John and Balbian sat outdoors in their favorite spot at the Café American drinking whiskey and smoking cigars, when John smirked and leaned over close to him.

"Uh!" Balbian said, sitting back, fanning the air with his hand. "Get away! The smell of your pomade is suffocating!"

"That's because the two women I'm going to see like it." John said with a suggestive chuckle. "And it's a date I do *not* want to break."

"But – what about Margaretha?"

"Could you, ah, keep her company this evening?" he said, suggestively.

"For God sakes, John! She's your wife!" Balbian gave him a disgusted look. He thought about it for a moment. "On second thought, maybe it's time I *did* meet her. I'd like to see what type of a girl would marry the likes of *you*."

"Be my guest." John said, thinking only of his impending liaison. He then smiled and got up and left the Café.

Balbian got up, left money on the table to pay their bill, then made his way to Tante Lavies's house.

On the doorstep, Balbian collected himself then pressed the doorbell.

He was momentarily stunned when Margaretha, about to turn 20 in just a couple of days, answered the door. Balbian found himself instantly charmed by the young woman.

"Good evening." He said with a slight bow. "My name is Johan de Balbian Verster. I am a friend of your husband's."

"The journalist for the *News of the Day*?" He nodded. "Come in, come in. John speaks of you often."

She gently closed the front door behind him as he stepped inside.

"I'm afraid John isn't here at the moment." She told him. "Would you like to wait for him in the parlor?"

Balbian entered the finely decorated room, noticing an elegant clock on the room's mantlepiece reading just after 7:00 o'clock. Margaretha entered and Balbian found himself completely captivated by the young woman.

"So, what happened." Bouchardon asked,

"As the evening wore on we engaged in conversation."

"Conversation. About what, may I ask?"

"Just about everything really - from the arts to languages. I even played the piano and sang for him."

"Is that all?"

"Mr. Balbian had originally planned to inform me of what John was up to - but found he just couldn't do it."

"And how do you know this?"

"He told me several years later when I chanced to meet him again."

"Did you know what your husband was doing?"

"Of course. John wasn't as clever as he thought he was."

"What happened next?"

The clock on the mantlepiece just finished chiming 10:00 o'clock when John walked into the parlor. Balbian watched as the man, posing as the perfect husband, lovingly kissing his wife - all the while winking to Balbian over her shoulder then sniffing his fingers.

Balbian, disgusted, walked out of the room passing close to John, giving him a dirty look. "I ought to kick you." He muttered.

Without another word Balbian donned his hat and walked out of the parlor into the front hallway – just as Louise was emerging down the interior stairs.

She paused for a moment, watching him exit the, then turned her attention to the parlor.

Louise stepped into the parlor's open doorway just as Margaretha pulled herself away from John – then slapped him across the face.

"How dare you kiss me!" She said, wiping her lips. "Especially when you still reek of cheap perfume!"

"He wouldn't have to seek the favor of women elsewhere," Louise said, making herself part of the conversation, "if *you* were a decent wife!"

"Always taking your brother's side, aren't you Tante Lavie?!" Margaretha told Louise. "Even when the bastard is whoring around on me!"

"You're just not good enough for my dear Rudolf!" Louise said, stepping over to John's side. "You know absolutely nothing about housekeeping."

"Don't you understand?!" Margaretha pleaded. "I'm not *meant* to be a housewife! I'm not inclined to frugality!"

"So what aspirations do you have?" Louise asked.

"I wish to be a dancer. And I simply refused to live a life without luxury."

Louise glanced at John, rolled her eyes then shook her head.

"Oh, how I longed to drift away from them." Margaretha told Bouchardon. "To float up to the bright lights where I belonged."

Bouchardon just glanced at the three men serving at the hearing, and said nothing.

"The tension between Tante Lavie and myself became so untenable," Margaretha continued, "John and I finally got a place of our own on Jacob Lennepkade, in Amsterdam."

"God, how wonderful it feels to be away from that prying shrew, Tante Lavie!" Margaretha said, stepping into her new home.

45

John pulled an envelope from their letterbox and opened it.

"Well?" Margaretha asked. "What does it say?"

"It seems," John said, reading the note, "that as brother of the Baroness, I, and my new wife, are invited to a reception at the Dutch Royal Palace to honor Queen Wilhelmina's upcoming sixteenth birthday."

Walking into the grand reception, Margaretha, resplendent in her long yellow wedding gown, arm in arm with John in his dress uniform accented with gold braid, displaying his medals, paused for a moment to take in the festivity of the room as men and women in their finest formal evening dress danced to the music of a live orchestra.

Margaretha shined – especially when everybody they met remarked on what a lovely couple they made.

"This was the life I envisioned!" Margaretha told Bouchardon. "Not staying at home, mending clothes and preparing paltry meals for my husband. High society was my natural milieu! Now it seemed we two were reconciled at last! Our marriage was not a mistake after all!"

Bouchardon studied Margaretha as she grew silent on the stand.

"Please tell the court what happened next."

"Within days of the event I was pregnant with our first child. I named him Norman John, in honor of the General."

"In March and again in September of 1896, John's sick leave was extended, each time for a period of six months."

"Why was that?"

"The first extension was due to another attack of rheumatism. The second because I became pregnant."

"Why should *you* being pregnant extend *his* sick leave?"

"My due date coincided at some point during our scheduled travel back to the Dutch East Indies – and I was not going to give birth somewhere at sea."

"Go on."

"Norman was born on January 30, 1897. Shortly afterwards, John received word that he'd been promoted to Major and was ordered back to Java."

"Did you celebrate his return to duty?"

"He did. He spent the next three months whoring around with the ladies of 'the ice skating club' while I stayed home alone, tending to my baby – and my skin sores."

"Skin sores?"

"Yes. The monster had given me syphilis." She said, leveling her gaze at Bouchardon. "Such a man should have been ashamed."

"Why?"

"His ruined body could only ruin other women..."

Chapter 5

"The young lieutenants pursue me and are in love with me."

❖   ❖   ❖

ON MAY 1, 1897, three months after Norman's birth, Margaretha and John sailed for the Dutch East Indies aboard the *SS Princes Amalia*. Standing at the railing of the ship as it leaves the harbor, her infant daughter in her arms, Margaretha is buoyant with excitement. In the moment, the twenty year's difference in their ages was of no concern whatever.

"Oh, Norman," She said to the baby, "This trip is going to be such an adventure! Just think of it - the Dutch East Indies – a whole new country..."

John proudly looked at his wife and son.

"You know," He said to Margaretha, leaning on the rail, "I have spent all my adult life in the tropics. The women I've known have mostly been natives. I cannot wait for you, my beautiful young wife, to cut an impressive figure at the garrison clubhouses."

Margaretha smiled, rocking and holding her baby close against the cool sea air.

The vast expanse of ocean faded into the small, barred window in her cell, her thoughts returning to her physical confinement. Sister Léonide, silently stood by, her hands clasped, intrigued by the melancholy of the story the woman told.

"So you moved to Java..."

Margaretha nodded, sighed, and continued her story.

"For a short while we lived in Ambarawa, a village south of Semarang in the center of Java. Then John was transferred to Toempoeng, near Malang, on the eastern side of the large island. It was a great improvement, believe me."

"Why was that dear?" Sister Léonide asked.

"Because Malang was a city with a lot of Europeans. I was no longer in a setting where white women were scarce – one might even say, at a premium."

Understanding her meaning, Sister Léonide nodded.

"We lived in Toempoeng for a year, during which time, my daughter Non was born, on May 2, 1898."

"Non? What an unusual name for a little girl..."

"It's a variation of the Malay word nonah, meaning 'young girl.' I always liked the sound of it."

"Ah."

"Anyway, with Johnnie now a Major and considered a prominent officer, we took up residence in a large house girdled by a wide verandah."

"It sounds beautiful."

"It was. Sometimes in the evening we'd stroll arm in arm through the lush parks maintained by our gardeners, looking back at the house with aristocratic pride as the servants lit the lamps one by one."

"Our weekly Saturday night visit to the officer's club was about our only form of entertainment. I always found myself surrounded by a score of young bachelor officers and planters. The young lieutenants pursued me and more than a couple of them told me they were in love with me."

"How brash."

"Even married men were not averse to flirting with me. After all, I was one of only a handful good looking young white women on the entire military post. I was, of course, flattered and flirted back. But I never let it go any further than that. Though, I must admit, it was difficult for me to behave in a way which gave my husband no cause for reproaches."

She sighed. "But, with the children taking up most of my time during the week, John soon took up drinking and visiting the native whores again. He'd come back home, begging my forgiveness, and promising never to do it again."

"Did you?"

"Yes. I forgave him, his bullying, his selfishness, and his indiscretions. And with my lapse in judgement, I soon found myself infected with syphilis – and pregnant again."

Sister Léonide shook her head.

"So, what did you do?"

"I hired a babu – a native woman to look after Norman - then joined a local theater troop."

"To celebrate Queen Wilhelmina's 18th birthday in the Spring of 1898, the theater troop put on a production of *The Crusaders*. I gracefully appeared on stage in a low cut purple velvet gown. Even as I walked onto the stage, I could hear a groan of lust followed by indiscreet remarks arise from the soldiers in the audience...

Even as Margaretha tries to perform her number, the whoops and cat calls increased to the verge of drowning her out. Incensed by the men's actions, John was quickly driven into a jealous rage. Dragging her by the hand, he yanked her off the stage during her performance, forcing her to run after him to avoid tripping as he hauled her out of the theater and back to their bungalow.

Later, soldiers passing their house could hear his angry bellows from their house, threatening Margaretha's life.

"Admit it!" He thundered. "You've slept with every one of them, haven't you?!"

"NO - I haven't – you pig!" She shouted back. "But I'm starting to wish I had! At least they'd know how to treat a woman - and not mount her like a bull in must!"

50

Enraged, John slapped her across the face with such force she was knocked to the floor.

The passing soldiers, having paused to listen to the altercation – and knowing full well what *he'd* been up to – could only shake their heads at his hypocrisy - then moved on.

Inside, as Margaretha grouped about on the floor, trying to shake off the blow, John looked around. Picking up a handy bread knife, he started to attack her with it.

Margaretha reached for the kitchen chair between them, pulling it over and tripping him, giving her time to stand up, find the front door and flee the house.

Scrambling to his feet, John stopped at the open door.

"Come back here, you bitch!" He shouted after her running figure as she fled down the dark pathway.

Margaretha paused and looked at Sister Léonide. "It was a scene, or something like it, we'd repeat every time he'd get drunk – and he got drunk a lot."

"I'm so sorry."

"Then John received his orders for transfer to the city of Medan."

"Medan? Where's that?"

"On Sumatra's east coast - opposite Malaya on the Strait of Malacca. He was promoted to the new garrison commander there, replacing one General Reisz. Then, two hours before we were to board the *SS Carpentier*, John rode out to Elsia's house on a horse."

"Elsia?"

"Yes, Mrs. Van Rheede - her husband Georg, was comptroller for the province."

"I see. Go on."

December 21, 1898

JOHN SAT ON his horse in front of the bungalow for a few moments as Elsia Van Rheed opened the screen door and stepped out on the porch. He addressed her without dismounting from his

51

saddle.

"My wife and children are coming to stay with you in a few hours until I get over to Medan." John said matter of factly. "You don't mind, do you?"

Elsia, never having liked the man, just looked at him.

"I won't have that mutt of yours!"

"All right." He said. "Blackie will come with me."

"Then no, I don't mind."

"Nor should you." He said. Without further niceties, he reigned in the horse and galloped away as Georg stepped out of the house.

"What was that all about?" Georg asked, watching John disappear down the road.

"Your skinflint commander just devised a way to put his wife and children up in a respectable household without spending any money."

"If you ask me, he's trying to keep Margaretha from meeting the new men."

"Regardless, she's ours to deal with now. I best make up the guest bedroom for her."

Later that day Margaretha, her infant and Norman arrived and moved into the Rheede home.

"Thank you for taking us in." Margaretha, cradling infant Nonnie in her arms, said to Elisa. "I realize this is an inconvenience."

"I understand." Elsia replied.

"I thought I was going with John – but at the last minute he said I had to stay behind to supervise the disposal of our furniture."

"Don't you just love how the Dutch government so freely issues transfers – but refuses to pay a penny for the moving of household goods?"

"I'm not really sure how to proceed..."

"Not to worry – I've been through this before." Elsia told her. "We'll sell everything at auction – then you can use the money to purchase new furniture when you get to Medan. Believe me, it's cheaper than paying for shipment over long distances out of pocket."

"Over his years in the Indies," Margaretha told Sister Léonide, "John went through an infinite number of transfers. It was a nightmare. We were constantly plagued by the financial burden the multiple auctions and purchases put on us."

March 28, 1899

WITH THE WARMER weather of spring and summer approaching, 22 year-old Margaretha, like many other white women on the base, now opted to wear the more comfortable native sarong and kabaja (skirt and blouse) instead of the heavier European clothing.

As John had failed to enclose any money for her support, over the last three months she had been forced to spend the money made from the auctioning of her furniture on herself and Norman.

This day she anxiously tore open the envelope of a new letter from John. Unfolding the single page letter, she let out a sigh when she realized that yet again, he had failed to send any money.

John's letter to Margaretha:

It's strange to see this city with its many multiple-storied homes and its excellent roads, electric lights, beautiful tokos (shops) that outshine those in Batavia, wonderful horses and carriages. They've had to kill 739 dogs during two days on account of rabies, but blackie is inside the house and feels fine.

And now, dear Griet, adieu! And be sure to give my regards to the Van Rheedes.

Your husband, John.

Margaretha turned to Elsia – and shook her head.

"What am I going to do?" She asked Elsia desperately. "I've received several letters from John – but again, he has not enclosed a cent. It is almost April and the situation is becoming quite embarrassing! Elsia - I am nearly out of money!"

"Not to fret – I'll write to my sister in Medan. I'll tell her to let John know his wife is broke and needs new clothes."

"Thank you."

Watching her walk away, Elsia starts writing the letter to her sister. After requesting the favor, she writes:

"I really feel sorry for Margaretha - intelligent, charming, always at a local club surrounded by admirers. She suffers so much from being married."

John's letter - April 24, 1899:

"You mention that having written me two letters you are waiting for my answer from Medan. Come now, Griet, I bet that by now you are laughing about your stupidity. 'To wait for an answer from Medan' – but Griet, that takes about sixteen days, and you mean to say that you intend not to write during all this time? That is really typical of you!"

"The thing that makes me so often inwardly complain in the fact that we absolutely never have any financial luck, and what a great many rotten things we have been obliged to do on account of all that lack of money."

"Who is that naval lieutenant you write about, who photographed the children and how did he happen to be in Toempoeng? You never explain things of that sort. Griet, and you can perfectly well understand that when I read this, I start thinking: 'Well now, who is that again? And how did he get to Toempoeng? It's funny – you suddenly jump from Jan Pik's (Norman's) sailor suit and Fluit's (Non's) affectionate nature to that lieutenant and then I do not hear a word about him anymore!

And so, Pik is very much in love with his little sister? That perpetual urge for kissing he certainly has from you."

"Yes Griet, just try to understand that when I rave and swear, this is caused principally because I am afraid for the children – for do not forget that our characters differ tremendously."

54

"John had been suspicious and jealous of me ever since he noticed I attracted men's attention on our honeymoon." She told Sister Léonide. "Over the years, while I matured and grew more attractive – he just aged - finally looking old enough to be my father."

Sister Léonide shook her head.

"It had been four months – going on five. Near the end of April, both Nonnie and Norman came down with something. I still have no idea what sickness it was, just that both of them remained under the weather for nearly a month before John finally made the necessary financial arrangements for our trip to Medan. He finally wrote to me and told me what to expect upon my arrival."

Johns letter May 14, 1899

"I'm glad to have received your letter of April 25, 1899, this morning, with your description of the children's illness. There is a lot of work waiting for you here, Griet, for these houses are dangerous to live in if one is not constantly busy with sweeping, moving flowerpots and tarring the premises, all kinds of vermin crawl around. Thus last night I saw a scorpion the size of which I had never before seen in my life. Although the bite of such a beast is not immediately fatal, it does cause a high fever and for small children it is very dangerous. Therefore you'll have to inspect the rooms everyday *yourself,* clean the children's beds and move the flowerpots.

"I am glad to note from your letter that you are perfectly aware of your heavy responsibility with the children and that you take care of them with devotion."

"As Chief Netherlands Military Officer," Margaretha explained, "John was required to host all the official receptions. The first of these was General Beisz' going-away party. And I must confess, Sister, I absolutely loved these functions."

Wearing an evening gown John had ordered all the way from Amsterdam, Margaretha glittered like a queen, standing arm in arm next to the army commander in his crisp uniform decorated with ribbons and medals.

But when older wives came to pay their respect, Margaretha refused to leave her husband's side.

"You supposed to approach and meet them halfway." John whispered to her.

"I will not."

"Why?"

"As the wife of the garrison commander, I feel it is the visitor's duty to come to me."

"But weren't most of the other wives older than you?"

"Age played no part in this. Of course, the fact that their husbands flocked around, flattering and flirting with me, didn't help."

"Pety jealousies being what they are, I'm sure it created an unpleasant situation for your husband..."

Late evening - June 27, 1899

"It's not enough that you insist on queening it over the other officer's wives!" John said to Margaretha angerly as they walked up to their darkened house. "You, the wife of the new garrison commander, have to flirt like a whore, turning their heads of their husbands as well!"

John stepped into the living room - to find the children's nurse, Babu, on the couch nearly naked and in a passionate embrace with one of the local native soldiers.

"What the hell is this?!" John thundered, becoming enraged and grabbing the man's shoulder, pulling him off the woman.

John then glanced at Babu, who immediately clutched her open gown closed. "You call this watching the children?!" He asked.

"Stop it!" Margaretha shouted to John. "I'm sure the children are fine."

"Sir!" The native soldier said, getting to his feet. "It is not her fault! I came to deliver that telegram." He pointed to an envelope sitting on an end table. "Our passion overwhelmed us. It will not happen again."

"You're damn right it won't!" John bellowed, stepping over to the end table. He quickly opened the envelope and read the missive inside.

"Get out!" John said, tossing the envelope back on the table. He then looked at Babu, reaching for her. "Come here you slut!"

The native man knocked John's hand away.

"Do not lay your filthy hands on her!" He said in a stern voice. "She is to be *my* wife!"

John suddenly turned his rage upon the man, slugging him again and again, beating the man savagely.

"John! Stop it!" Margaretha pleaded, getting in between them. "You're killing him!"

John held his punch and stood back. The native soldier leveled his gaze at John, wiping his bloodied mouth on his sleeve. Then clutching his bruised ribs, slowly got to his feet as Babu ran to his side and helped him up.

"Get out!" John shouted at the native soldier. "Get out of my house! And *do not* come back!"

Babu glanced at Margaretha, who with an openhanded gesture, then pointing, indicated it would be all right – but he had to go.

The native soldier made his way out of the house as Babu collected herself and hurried upstairs to the children's room. Margaretha turned and looked at her husband.

"John – they weren't doing anything we haven't done! What are you so mad at?"

He just flashed Margaretha a dirty look then picked up the envelope. "It's General Biesz!" He said, throwing her the telegram. "You remember how you acted towards his wife at the party... Well, he informed me this morning I am *not* being promoted to lieutenant colonel! Not now – not ever!"

"I'm so sorry..." She handed it back to him.

"You should be!" He looked at the telegram. "Now, it says here I am being transferred back to Java." He wadded up the paper and tossed it aside. As the anger grew inside of him, he looked at Margaretha – then.

57

"And it is all *your* fault!" He shouted, slapping her across the face, knocking her to the floor.

Clutching her throbbing cheek, Margaretha got to her feet as John walked away.

Babu then anxiously called to her from the top of the stairs.

"The children!" She said with a quiver in her voice. "There is something wrong!"

Ignoring her pain, Margaretha immediately ran up the stairs, taking two at a time, and rushed to the children's room.

Seeing them and overhearing Babu, John instantly sent for Dr. Roelfsema, who was medical officer for that part of the Preanger Province.

Once in the room, Margaretha found Norman and Non retching in pain as they vomited ropes of thick black liquid.

"Call the doctor!" Margaretha ordered.

"He's on his way!" John assured her as they tried to comfort and care for the children.

It was long after dark before the tired doctor, now cleaning his hands on a towel, took Margaretha and John aside.

"I've done all I could." Dr. Roelfsema said to them. "At least they're resting quietly now."

"What is wrong with them?" Margaretha asked.

Dr. Roelfsema, hesitant to ask her a delicate question, looked through his medical bag.

"Well?" John asked.

The doctor paused and looked directly at him.

"They've ingested some kind of poison. Children can do that – eat something they're not supposed to – I've seen it before."

"But Norman's just two and a half years-old and she's an infant! How could they... Can't you give them something to counteract it!"

"Not without knowing what they took in the first place. If I give them the wrong thing..." Dr. Roelfsema threw his hands in the air in frustration.

"What are their chances?" John asked him. "I want the truth."

"I think your daughter just might make it. She's tough."

"What about my son?!"

"If he makes it through the night, then he has a good chance."

"No!" John wailed, dropping to knees at Norman's bedside. "Please, God!" he said, tears running down his cheeks, clasping his hands in prayer. "Save my son!"

Margaretha glanced at Dr. Roelfsema who, catching her eye, shook his head slightly.

June 28, 1899

The first light of the next morning found John prostrate over the bed of his deceased son. Margaretha sat on the edge of her daughter's bed. Dr. Roelfsema stood bent over the daughter with a stethoscope to Non's chest, checking her breathing.

"Your one year-old daughter is barely hanging on – but her heart sounds strong." The doctor said to Margaretha. "I believe she just might make it."

Dr. Roelfsema turned to John.

"I don't mean to be indelicate, Commander, but with this climate and all – its best we bury your son as soon as possible."

John nodded, got to his feet, wiped his eyes and collected himself.

"Send my aide in here."

A man appeared at the door to the room and snapped to attention. "Sir?"

"Yes Lieutenant – my son Norman will be put to a dignified rest this afternoon - with *full* military honors – all the pomp and splendor. Make it happen."

"Yes sir."

"And Lieutenant – inform *all* the officers of the garrison that they *will* be attending."

"Yes sir!"

The Lieutenant saluted then turned and left.

It was then John noticed the calendar sitting on an end table. Tearing off the leaves for June 27 and June 28 he carefully folded them and tucked them into his shirt pocket. He also cut a lock from the boy's hair just as two soldiers appeared with a stretcher to take Norman away.

"Do they really need that?" Margaretha asked, pointing to the stretcher. "He's not even three years old..."

"Shut up, Bitch!" John said to her. "He'll be treated like any other dead soldier." He turned to the two orderly's. "Proceed."

Margaretha shook her head and watched as, with great ceremony, they lifted the toddler's small body onto the stretcher then exited the room.

MARGARETHA ENTERED the base chapel that afternoon to find John, in full uniform, standing in front of Norman's casket, tears welling in his eyes.

"Oh God! Why me?!" John wailed, throwing himself across the boy's coffin. "How could you let this happen to me?!"

"You know the doctor suspects foul play." Margaretha told him as she approached. "Let him do an autopsy – and find out for sure."

"No!" he said, thumping his fist on the casket. He stood, collecting himself and turning to Margaretha and looking her in the eye.

"I've heard the rumors that Babu poisoned my boy – but I don't believe a word of them! Why would she do that?! Because I embarrassed her boyfriend? Ridiculous!"

His face twisted into anger as he studied her for a moment.

"No," He said, pointing at her, "It was *you* who killed our baby boy!"

"What?!"

"I remember how ill he and Nonnie looked the day they arrived in Medan!" He clutched her shoulders and shook her. "Admit it! You abandoned him in Toempoeng so you could go whoring!"

"How can you say that?!" Margaretha sobbed, breaking free of his grasp. "Can't you see this is killing me too?!"

"Go to hell, bitch!" He said, stomping out of the church.

As Norman's casket was lowered into the ground later that afternoon, John and Margaretha had only to share a glance to let it be known they no longer were bothering to disguise their mutual disgust and hatred for each other.

I N HIS HUT, the native soldier and Babu, sharing a bed that night, their room nestled in darkness, watched as the last of the workmen from the funeral, having covered the grave, finally filtered from the cemetery and started back to their homes.

Soon, only the sounds of the jungle night could be heard through the open windows. Babu snuggled up to her lover in the bed to find he was laying there with one arm behind his head, wide awake.

"What is wrong?" Babu asked.

"The Major's kids."

"What about them?"

"You were the only person to have access to them..."

Babu moved away from him, and sat up. "Are you asking if I poisoned them?"

"Well, did you?"

Babu climbed out of bed, pulling a light-weight robe over her naked body, lit up a cigarette then began pacing the room as she talked.

"All right – yes. Yes I did." She said defiantly.

"But why?"

"Why? Because of what McLeod did to you! The beating, the humiliation you suffered – all for nothing! Because he is nothing but a bully!"

"But the boy..."

"He was sickly anyway." She paused her pacing and looked directly at her husband. "Oh, how McLeod doted on that child! "He is everything to me!" he declared more than once. So, the cruelest form of revenge was to destroy something he loved!"

"And you did this – for *me*?"

"Not just for you, my love. *I* crave McLeod's pain!"

"But why?"

She paused, taking a drag on the cigarette. "I didn't want to tell you this – but when he first transferred here – before we met - he ap-

61

proached me and we quickly became lovers. But the moment his wife stepped foot on this island he threw me over like so much trash."

"You'll take care of my children!" He snarled when his family arrived. "And you won't bother me again!"

He reached out to her, pulling her back onto the bed. She flicked the cigarette away.

"So, he was punishing you by beating me when he found us?" He asked, pulling her close.

She nodded. "So, you see – I had no choice." She said, wrapping her arms around him. "I had to punish him far, far worse than he'd injured you."

"Yes." He said, looking her in the eyes in the moonlight. "Yes, you did."

Embracing, the couple rolled over into the darkened shadows.

Chapter 6

"His faithlessness freed me..."

❖   ❖   ❖

MARGARETHA STEPPED from their newly arrived carriage and looked around at the Willem I Military Establishment on Java. A second Lieutenant was waiting there to greet them. "Where do we live?" She asked the soldier.

"You will find housing in the kampong[5] of Banjoe Biroe."

"Certainty not what I'd call a tropical paradise." John told him. "Look around - one has nothing to look at but the mountains. Without an almanac one would not even know what day it is... Sundays here are absolutely miserable. People who have a suicidal tendency could easily put it into practice on a day like that."

"I admit," Margaretha told the Sister, "that at night it was incredibly quiet there - with only a badly functioning lantern spreading uncertain twilight at the crossroads. That first night we had an invasion of butter-flies, plus flying ants and termites. The millions of little insects about drove us crazy!"

---

[5] native village

"I discovered," Margaretha told Sister Léonide, "that a good many Dutch enlisted men cohabitated with their Javanese wives or mistresses in the villages that surrounded the base."

"Do you believe John kept a paramour?"

"I *know* he did. I even met her once." Margaretha straightened herself up. "Where do you think he acquired the syphilis he infected me with? After going through the mercury treatments, I refused to engage in sex with him ever again."

"I can't imagine that created a very healthy atmosphere for your marriage."

Margaretha shrugged. "What marriage? Why he ever placed that ad is beyond me. And things only went down-hill from there."

The Ides of March 1900

"I'm afraid Margaretha is suffering an attack of typhoid fever." Dr. Roelfsema told John at her bedside. "You should have called me earlier - her condition has worsened now to the point that she is in endless misery."

"But she'll still be able to nurse and attend to Non – right?"

"God no!" Dr. Roelfsema replied indignantly. "Margaretha's much too ill to do any of that. Commander, your daughter's care now falls squarely upon your shoulders!"

"What?! How am *I* supposed to nurse her?!"

"Bottled milk, of course."

"Okay - how much?"

"She should be fed every two hours – I'd say about five bottles a day."

"What?! Five bottles of milk - a *day*?! But they're thirty cents each! It'll break me!" John looked a Margaretha. "This is all your fault!" He shouted, kicking her bed. "You bitch!"

Non began crying. Dr. Roelfsema put himself between John and the bed.

"Blame God if you need a scapegoat!" He said. "Right now, your wife is fighting for her life and your daughter's upset and hungry – and

64

it's up to *you* to take care of her! Or should I just take her to the orphanage so you're no so inconvenienced?"

John gave Dr. Roelfsema a long dirty look – then stepped over and picked up his daughter.

"Listen Commander - I have no specific feeling of friendship, nor enmity for either you or your wife. Yet, during the time I've known Margaretha, her conduct - notwithstanding the many rude insults she's had to endure in public from you - has been perfectly correct.

"She could have grown into a good wife and mother - if only *you* had been more equable and sensible man! As it is, your marriage is doomed to failure!"

With that, Dr. Roelfsema grabbed his satchel and left.

John looked at Margaretha while rocking his daughter in his arms and shook his head. "Bitch." He said.

"It wasn't until May 20th that I was well enough to travel." Margaretha told the Sister.

"You were lucky. I have seen the suffering one goes through with that disease. Many do not survive."

"I was sent to Kemloko - a coffee plantation on the slopes of a volcano at Kroewoek - to recuperate while John continued to care for Nonnie." She glanced at the Sister. "During my illness John had changed and become withdrawn. He openly visited the native whores - blamed me for Norman's death. His pet name for me was now 'that bitch.' And whenever our son was brought up, tears came to his eyes. He even told me 'the loss of that wonderful little boy has cracked something inside of me which will always remain there.'"

Sister Léonide shook her head.

"Arriving at Kemloko, I introduced myself to Louise and Laura Balkstra, the daughters of the man that owned the plantation, as Gertha, to symbolize a change and a new identity. For John's faithlessness freed me - gave me license, if you will, to pursue my own pleasure."

"I'm afraid I outraged their mother, though - always flirting with men. Indeed - I began sneaking away with one of them, Monbrun was his name. I'd return to them later all disheveled. Louise once told me she could always tell when I'd been with a man. She said she could see a serene secret shining in the depths of my eyes – like hidden treasure just out of reach."

"They once told me I had splendid legs - and danced like a goddess."

"What did you say?"

"I told them that one day I would be celebrated - or notorious."

"Why on earth did you tell them that?"

Margaretha shrugged. "I just felt it within me."

"By the time I returned to John at the end of the summer, I could see that our relationship was over. He now blamed me for being passed over for promotion to lieutenant colonel."

"That's absurd. And just how were you to blame, dear?"

"I asked him that very question – but never got an answer."

Sister Léonide shook her head again. "You were such an unhappy couple..."

"It was October 2, 1900, that my 44 year-old husband decided to resign from the army. Having been a soldier for twenty-eight years, he was entitled to a full annual pension of 2800 guilders. We went to live at Sindanglaja, a small village between Buitenzorg and Bandung. The mountain climate here was healthy and life was fairly cheap – a lot cheaper than in Holland – which was the main reason we stayed on in the tropics."

Margaretha sighed. "But our relationship had become intolerable. There was hardly a day that our tempers didn't flair and our voices were not raised in bitter arguments."

"Here I was - in my early 20's, living in a small village in the Indies with hardly enough money to get by – and living with a much older husband whom I no longer liked. I was fed up with army life. It was at this time I began hounding him about returning to Amsterdam – maybe visiting Paris."

"What did John say about that?"

"He yelled at me. He said 'What the hell! If you want that much to go to Paris – why don't you just go and leave me alone!'"

Margaretha laughed.

"Another time, at the party of a mutual friend, I was dancing while he was talking on the sidelines. Passing close by with my dancing partner, I said:

"Hello Darling."

"You can go to hell, bitch!" he replied.

"Hey! That is no way to address a lady." Her dancing partner replied, confronting John.

"Lady?!" John said so loudly that everyone turned and looked at him. "Ha! My wife is a stinking wretch! She's a bloodsucking beast who has the totally depraved nature of a scoundrel!"

"You forget yourself, sir! You are no longer the commander!"

"You want her?! Take her! I chuckle all over when I think that someone else might marry her! Go ahead – you'll only to find out that you sold yourself down the river – just like I did!"

"Shut up!" Margaretha shouted at John. "You snake!" She turned to her dance partner. "You should see him at home with his red bloodshot eyes - drunk and spiteful! He spits at me then threatens me with a loaded revolver! Or hits me and dares me to strike back!"

"Shut up, bitch!"

"You have given me a distaste for matters sexual such as I cannot forget! I just wish one day I would become a widow!"

John moved as if to attack her – when her dance partner intervened, standing between them.

"To get to her – you'll have to go through me first."

"Well? What happened?"

"There was a time John would have fought him. But time and the military had taken its toll - he wasn't a young man anymore."

John backed off, then spit on the floor. "Take her!" He said. "Everyone else has! You're welcome to the bitch."

"March 19, 1902, marked John's twenty-fifth year in the military. Now he was eligible for a full pension. Sick of the tropics, he decided to move back to Holland. He told me I could come along or stay where I was – either way *he* was taking Nonnie with him."

"John's abusive behavior to me aboard the *SS Konongin Wilhelmina* all the way home made me almost wish I'd stayed in the Indies." Margaretha sighed. "Of course, once back in Holland, we were broke and forced to moved in with Tante Lavies again."

"I simply could not stand that horrible woman! I began coming home late for dinner every night just to avoid her! His sister (and he agreed) the real reason I was coming home late was because I was whoring around and flaunting myself in public."

"We took an apartment of our own at 188 Breestraat in Amsterdam - a nice part of town. But no longer under the protection of his sister's title, John's creditors now began to bring lawsuits. Remember Mr. Calisch?"

"The man your husband borrowed three thousand guilders from six years earlier? And whom he had asked you to "be nice" to?"

Margaretha nodded. "It turned out he was only one of *many* persons looking for the return of their money. We were besieged with legal letters and house visits by solicitors all summer."

"It became so bad that when came home the afternoon of August 28, I found the apartment empty. Our marriage collapsed completely that day. John had pulled up stakes and left - taking all his clothes and personal belongings - and 4½ year-old Nonnie - with him."

"I found out from his journalist friend, J. T. Z. de Balbian Verster, John had fled from me and his creditors by moving to a friend's house in Velp, near Arnhem."

"I immediately traveled to Arnhem to retrieve my daughter, staying with one of John's cousins, Madame Goodvriend nee Baroness Sweerts de Landas. When John refused to see me or even let me see Non, I filed for a legal separation. It was granted three days later by the Amsterdam tribunal entirely in my favor."

"Only three days?" Sister Léonide asked. "What did you tell them?"

"The truth. That he beat me almost daily - referred to me to others as "That bitch of mine!" That when he was drunk he shouted at me: "I will make your life so miserable that you will bugger off!" And once thrashed me with a walking stick until the maidservant had to intervene. I requested the court to grant me a divorce with the provision he give me a monthly payment of one hundred guilders and I would come live with Madame Goodvriend nee Baroness Sweerts de Landas in Arnhem."

"Well, at least you were able to keep your daughter and collect one hundred guilders a month alimony."

Margaretha laughed. "Claiming poverty, He never paid me a penny. If fact, he placed an advertisement in the *Arnhem Daily* requesting all and sundry "not supply any goods to my estranged wife, Margaretha McLeod-Zelle."

"He didn't!"

"He certainly did! He then demanded that, as I had *so* disgraced the family name, Madame Goodvriend must kick me to the streets - so she did. I found myself with no money, no friends, and living on the streets of Arnhem."

"How on earth did you survive, dear?"

Margaretha took a deep breath and looked at the Sister. "This prison is filled with women in that same situation who were forced to survive."

"You mean - by entertaining gentlemen in *maisons de rendez-vous...*"

"Believe me, I was not entertained – and they were *not* gentlemen. But it did allow me to survive. I didn't know how, but I fully intended to get Nonnie back."

Chapter 7

"If I were to be successful I was going to have to dance."

❖   ❖   ❖

MARGARETHA STOOD UP, stepping over to the barred window in her cell. Looking out, she momentarily lost herself among the clouds in the overcast sky. She then sighed and turned back to Sister Léonide.

"My uncle Taconis sent me enough money to come live with him in The Hague. There I got a job modeling clothes as a mannequin for brief time. Once I had saved up some money I fully intended to get Nonnie back." Margaretha sighed. "All I ever wanted was Nonnie to live with me so I could be a decent mother. Without her, I felt lost. I was abstaining from everything for my child."

"This was it! I was tired of fighting against life. I finally begged John's cousin, Edward, to help me make one last attempt to regain custody of my daughter. I made it clear to him that if John didn't live up to his duties – and in the event that I was certain of never again being able to have Non with me as her mother - then I would care no longer and cast *everything* aside!"

"Am I to understand your efforts were in vain?"

Margaretha nodded. "It was only after I finally realized John was *never* going to pay me and that I would never see my daughter again, that I decided to leave Holland and start a new life in Paris."

"Why Paris?"

Margaretha shrugged. "I thought all women who ran away from their husbands went to Paris. Besides, when I was there with my husband, I saw how the rich men in top hats flaunted their mistresses on the Champs Elysées. I was not blind to how John was mesmerized by the high-kicking women doing the Can-Can at the Moulin Rouge and Folies Bergère."

" *You* wanted to be part of these high society salonnières."

"I thought I did. But I quickly discov-
ered it was all just a glittering façade."

"I was 27 years-old when I took the train and arrived in Paris without any money and without any clothes. But I had a good figure. So, claiming to be the wid- ow of a Dutch East Indies soldier, trying to support myself and two children, I be- gan posing nude for such painters as Edouard Bisson, Octave Denis Victor Guillemet, and Fernand Cormon. And for a few months all went well."

Margaretha looked at Sister Léonide.

"But then a snobbish but influential artist told me I was "not up to specifications.""

"What did he mean by 'specifications'?"

Margaretha blushed. "My small bust size. He told me 'A woman is supposed to be voluptuous!' My bookings suddenly dwindled into al- most nothing."

"Destitute - missing my child, my house, and my comfort - I was forced to resort to sleeping with men for pay." Margaretha looked at the Sister. "Please don't think me bad at heart!" She pleaded. "I did it only out of poverty."

71

"I returned to Holland on March 28, 1904, defeated, and broke. But my father and his wife wanted nothing to do with me, so I stayed with one of John's uncles in Nijmegen. But as soon as John learned of my whereabouts, the hateful man insisted that no assistance be given me. After only one week I was forced to leave."

"Desperate and penniless, for the next two months I again reduce myself to prostitution to survive. Finally, in June, with nothing to keep me in Holland, and with only half a Franc in my pocket, I again left for Paris – this time for good."

"Upon arriving, at the train station I happened to notice an advertising poster for the Circus Molier featuring a scantily clad trick rider. It reminded me that while in the Indies, I had become a skilled horsewoman. I went straight to the Circus - gave a brief demonstration of my riding to its owner, Monsieur Molier – and left with a job as a trick rider."

"That same day?"

Margaretha smiled and nodded.

"I was not shy about riding a large white horse wearing – how shall I say it – next to nothing – and the act proved very successful. By the end of the summer, large crowds filled the tent each time I went on."

Margaretha sighed, going over her history in her mind.

"I'd been doing the act for about nine months when the circus owner came to me..."

"I've been watching you." Monsieur Molier said to her as he looked her over. "You know, with a face and body like yours, you'd be a lot more successful as an exotic dancer than you'll ever be riding these horses."

Margaretha found the idea intriguing. "I never gave dancing any thought..."

"You know only too well that you're beautiful and attract the attentions of men." He continued. "And you know how to be charming. A great many women have started with a lot less."

"When on my honeymoon," She told him, "I saw how the rich men in top hats flaunted their mistresses on the Champs Elysées. I was

72

not blind to how they, and John, were mesmerized by the high-kicking women doing the Can-Can at the Moulin Rouge and Folies Bergère."

"They've got waiting lists a kilometer long of girls wanting to be on the chorus lines. No, if you really want to be successful, you're going to need a new angle – something different that will draw the people in. Got any ideas?"

"Well," She said, thinking. "I've never done any professional dancing in my life – but when I was in Java and Sumatra, I remember watch-

 ing some of the native women perform *their* dances. I even speak conversational Malay."

"I can see your name in lights now," Monsieur Molier said, envisioning a theater marquee. "Lady Gresha McLeod - Native of Java - performing the sacred, holy dances from the mystical East!"

"You can put together a costume from the circus' collection of clothing and accessories!"

"You want me to dance here?"

"No, no. Ever hear of Madame Kiréesky?" He asked.

Margaretha shook her head.

"She's a friend of mine – a singer who is a hostess, active in Paris society. She also organizes benefit performances. If you're willing, I can arrange for you to dance in one of these."

Margaretha smiled. "Okay."

"And while putting together a costume, see if you can concoct a back-story for Lady Gresha."

"What do you mean?"

"You know, her history - about how, in her youth, she had been initiated in the sacred dances of the Buddhist temples in the far east – that sort of thing. It will give your act a certain - mystique - not found with the other women dancers."

"I understand."

February 4, 1905

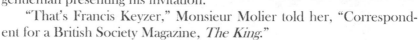

MARGARETHA and Monsieur Molier watched from behind the stage curtain as the specially invited guests appeared at the door. Only after showing their invitations, were they allowed to step inside and find a seat.

"Who is that man?" Margaretha asked, pointing to the well-dressed gentleman presenting his invitation.

"That's Francis Keyzer," Monsieur Molier told her, "Correspondent for a British Society Magazine, *The King*."

"And the man behind him?"

"Monsieur Emile Ètienne Guimet. He's an industrialist who turned to collecting on a grand scale. He's considered an expert on all things eastern. Just to house his private collection, he had the Museum of Oriental Art built on the Place d'Iéna."

After the private audience was in its place, Margaretha as Lady Gresha, appeared from behind the curtain. Laden with perfume and an elaborate costume of jewels, precious metals, a casque of worked gold on her head, an intricate breastplate beneath her arms, a transparent white robe, and a scarf about her hips, she glided in.

For a moment she stood motionless, amid a mass of flowers, transfixed, her eyes fastened on a statue of Shiva.

Then - in building undulating, hypnotic, tiger-like movements - as if striving to find favor with the god - she slowly approached the statue.

Monsieur Guimet found himself held spellbound by the rhythmic undulating dancer. Her eyes shining fire, she became more frenzied, more feverish, throwing off the flowers and the veils one by one - until finally, in a state of frenzy, she unclasped the belt that held the scarf about her hips - and in a swoon collapsed naked at Shiva's feet!

The next dance was equally impressive. She stood before them as a

graceful young girl, a *slendang* (the veil worn by Javanese maidens) around her waist. In her hand she held a passion-flower, and she danced to it "with all the gladness of her sunny nature. But the flower was enchanted, and under its charm she loses command of herself and slowly unwinds the *slendang*. As the veil drops to the ground, consciousness returns. She is ashamed and covers her face with her hands."

"My God!" Monsieur Guimet exclaimed, jumping to his feet. "Lady McLeod is Venus!"

Both Guimet and his director, Monsieur de Milloué, were completely captivated by the performance. So much so, that Guimet decided on the spot to treat his friends to a special demonstration of her oriental art.

"Lady McLeod," Monsieur Guimet asked, "Would you do me the honor of dancing at the Musée Guimet?"

"Is that the museum of Oriental art I've heard about?"

"It is indeed. I'm positive your sacred dance of the East will attract an audience of the elite! Paris' wealthiest aristocrats!"

Margaretha smiled. "Is it for the sacred dance – or the nudity?"

"Perhaps a little of both."

"All right, Monsieur Guimet."

"I have but one suggestion," he stated, "You need a better stage -name – something as intriguing as your performance."

"I was considering that myself." She told him. "What do you think of Mata Hari?"

"Mata Hari... I like it. It sounds mysterious. Does it have a meaning?"

"It's a Malay phrase meaning Eye of the Day – you know – the sun. I remember hearing it when I first moved to Java."

Six hundred of the wealthy elite of Paris received invitations for a show at the Musée scheduled for March 13, 1905 in the museum's domed library now transformed into an Indian temple. Flowers and vines coiled around the eight columns supporting the dome, each column topped by statues of bare-breasted women. An atmosphere of

76

mystery was created with the entire scene being illuminated only by the light of countless candles. Floodlit in the background stood a three-foot high, four armed Siva Nataraja from southern India, surrounded by a circle of flames - it was one of Monsieur Guimet's most prized 11th century bronze statues.

An off-scene orchestra played music inspired by Hindu and Javanese melodies as Mata Hari, wearing a white cotton brassiere covered with Indian-type jewel-studded breastplates, emerged onto the scene surrounded by four black-togaed girls.

"Bracelets of similar design were worn on her wrists and upper arms, while her head supported an Indian diadem that curled up backwards above her black hair, knotted *à l'espagnole.* Jeweled bands were clasped around her waist holding up a sarong which from the hollow of her back descended around her hips toward a point on her belly about half-way down below the navel."

Sitting around her, the Nautsches exited her further uttering terrible "stâ-stâ-stâ" sounds as Mata Hari, gasping for breath, sank down at the feet of the god – where her dancing girls covered her with a golden sheet. Then, without any feeling of shame, she got up gracefully, pulled the holy veil around her, and kindly thanking both Siva and the Parisians, walked off amidst thunderous bravos!

77

Afterwards, Margaretha, now dressed in an elegant evening gown, joined the public, and playing with a Javanese *wajong* puppet which she held in her hands, told the audience the story of the prehistoric drama of Adjurnah.

The next day, the Paris newspaper critics outdid themselves in find-ing words of praise extolling her passion, her performance, and announcing her triumph. In *The Press* Henri Ferrare raved, "her face makes a strange foreign impression." "Her dance "personifies all of the poetry of India – its mysticism, its voluptuousness, its charm – a really paradise-like dream."

The Gallic: "Mata Hari is so feline, extremely feminine, majestically tragic, her body's thousand curves and movements trembling in a thousand rhythms."

The Flash: "An exotic spectacle, yet deeply austere. Mata Hari's flexible body takes on the shape of the undulations of flames, then suddenly freezes like the wavy edge of a Kris."

La Presse: "She dances with veils, bejeweled brassieres and that is about all. She wears the dress of the bayadere with incomparable grace.

"From Java, on the burning soil of which island she grew up, she brings an unbelievable suppleness and a magic charm, while she owes her powerful torso to her native Holland.

"No one before her has dared to remain like this with trembling ecstasy and without any veils in front of the god - and with what beautiful gestures, both daring and chaste!

"She is indeed Absaras, sister of the Nymphs, the Naiads and the Valkyrie, created by Sundra for the perdition of men and sages.

"Mata Hari does not only act with her feet, her arms, eyes, mouth, and crimson fingernails. Mata Hari, unhampered by any clothes, plays with her whole body. And then, when the gods remain unmoved by the offer of her beauty and youth, she offers them her love, her chastity – one by one her veils, symbols of feminine honor, fall at the feet of the god. But Siva wants even more. Devidasha gets closer to him – one more veil, a mere nothing – and erect in her proud and victorious nudity, she offers the god the passion which burns in her."

When *The New Vienna Journal* declared: "Isadora Duncan is dead! Long live Mata Hari!" other newspapers quickly responded, creating a rivalry, comparing her with all the celebrity dancers of the day, such as Maud Allan.

The Gallic called her performance "far from the entrechats of our classic dancers."

Parisian Life described her act more succinctly. "She wears the costume of the bayadère, as much simplified as possible, and toward the end she simplifies it even a little more."

"The following evening, March 15," Margaretha told Sister Leonide, "As Mati Hari I continued my conquest of French society during another concert again organized by Madame Kiréevsky.

"On May 5, 1905, I was invited to dance in the garden of Miss Natalie Clifford Barney, an American expatriate author known as "The Amazon of Letters."

It was extremely cold that spring day in Neuilly and Margaretha made her appearance nude sitting on a white horse. Contrary to what the crowd expected, Mata Hari's skin was not dark, but quite purple. Greatly exposed on her white horse, the dancer had turned numb with the cold.

There's an intruder in the house!

"My second performance at Natalie Barney's took place indoors. Again, I agreed to appear entirely in the nude – but on the strict condition that only women be present."

"One of the women invited was Ms. Dorothy Rockhill, an American who had married a young British violinist, Arthur Larkin. Ms. Rockhill refused to accept the invitation if her husband was not included. They thought they could fool me by dressing the man in women's clothes. But once on stage, I spotted that wolf in sheep's clothing right off."

"There is an intruder in the house!" Margaretha shouted, lunging at him with an outstretched spear that had been added to her war dance. The man clamored to his feet and ran from the room nearly frightened to death.

While the French and British press praised Mata Hari as a bold and daring dancer, Holland was somewhat more conservative, as even sunbathing was still strictly separated according to the sexes.

A Dutch correspondent for the *Nieuwe Rotterdamsche Courant* of May 31, 1905, met her in Paris.

"I visited the mysterious woman in the boarding house where she lived near the Champs Élysées, in a room overflowing with flowers – flowers everywhere – a forest of flowers in large costly bouquets.

"She is a tall and slender chic young woman, beautiful, with dark complexion, dressed in a smart suit, straw hat with dark red flowers, who smiles, talks, who moves gracefully and with ease through the room – Mata Hari!"

"Think of it- from an obscure Dutch girl, forced to sell her body just to feed herself, I, as Mata Hari, was now the talk of the town!"

"That is something."

"During that year, I danced over thirty times at the most exclusive salons of Paris - plus six times at the Trocadero Theater. That's where arrangements were made to represent, as closely as possible, the atmosphere of the Guimet Museum. You know, oriental carpets, palm trees, flowers, and incense burners.

"I danced three times at the home of Baron Henri de Rothschild, at the home of Cécile Sorel, at the Grand Cercle. That's where I shared the program with Lina Cavalieri."

"The famous soprano?"

Margaretha nodded. "I danced my way all across Europe - Paris, Berlin, Madrid, Monte Carlo, Vienna - in exclusive salons and in private homes, such as Baron de Rothschild's and Gaston de Menier's."

"After each performance I donned an evening gown, and having perfect knowledge of how to behave in high society, I would easily mingle with my hosts and their guests.

"I knew the public was erotically fascinated. And, as the dancer's mystique swelled, I expanded her background story. I even told the press Mati Hari was the daughter of a temple dancer in India, rescued by a Scottish lord.[6]"

Sister Léonide shook her head in disbelief.

Margaretha sighed. "But I missed my daughter. Since separating from John, I saw Non only once in 1903. She was 4-years-old. Then I learned John had separated from his second wife. Their daughter, Norma, remained with her mother. Why then couldn't my daughter, Non, come and live with me in Paris?"

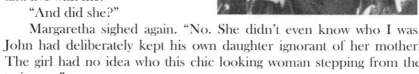

"I made an appointment with John to meet Non, at the Arnhem railway station."

"You just wanted to see her?"

"Truth be told, now that I was doing well and money was no longer a concern, my intention was to see if Non would come and live with me."

"And did she?"

Margaretha sighed again. "No. She didn't even know who I was. John had deliberately kept his own daughter ignorant of her mother! The girl had no idea who this chic looking woman stepping from the train was."

---

[6] These statements would later confuse reckless researchers who took them as fact for Margaretha's history.

"How would you like to come with me?" Margaretha asked the now 7-year-old.

"If Daddy allows me to..."

John scowled, looking Margaretha in the eye.

"Daddy does *not!*" He said sternly, taking Non by the hand. Margaretha had tears welling in her eyes, as he led her from the train station and she helplessly looked on.

"But I was determined to get her back – kidnap her if necessary. I worked out a plan with my maid, Anna. She was to go to Velp, a small town near Arnhem where John lived, not far from the German border. Anna was to take up watch in the neighborhood of Non's school, posting another person at the school's exit. This person would signal her when Non was approaching, and point her out. Anna had brought some candy along to keep the girl interested. She was to then take Non by car to Antwerp and continue from there by train to Paris."

Margaretha looked at Sister Leonide. "Wouldn't you know it – John would pick this day to come and fetch his daughter."

Anna had just taken Non by the hand when she sited John - and panicked.

"You there!" John said, rushing up to Non. "What are you doing with my daughter?!"

"I, uh..."

"Go on – explain yourself!"

"I was just telling your daughter that a lady gave me a present to give to her."

John was immediately suspicious.

"If presents are to be given," He said gruffly in a commanding officer's voice, "I'll be the one to give them!" with that he stalked off with Non, leaving Anna standing there with a red face. Not knowing what else to do, Anna caught the first train back to Paris.

"It turns out I was never to see my daughter again." Margaretha glanced at Sister Leonide. "May I ask a favor?"

The Sister studied her for a moment then nodded her head.

"When all the letters started pouring in and the newspaper articles appeared at the beginning of my career as Mata Hari, at night in my hotel room I carefully pasted them into my scrapbooks."

The Sister gave her a questioning look.

"I want to give the books to my daughter – but I since my arrest I don't know what's happened to them. I have the feeling I will not be leaving here anytime soon. Could you find them for me?"

Sister Leonide patted her hand. "I will see what I can do." She assured her.

Chapter 8

"One would need new words to explain...Mata Hari."

❖   ❖   ❖

"I MET MAÎTRE Clunet in July of 1905." Margaretha told the Sister at their next meeting. "He was a civil lawyer, twenty years older than myself. We had a brief affair and has remained my true and trusty friend. After I professed my aspirations to him one night, he sent me, with a warm word of recommendation, to a friend of his, Gabriel Astruc, one of the best-known impresarios in Paris..."

July - 1905

27 YEAR-OLD Margaretha walked into the booking agent's office to see a middle-aged man sitting at his desk, looking through headshots of various show folk while smoking a cigar.

"I was told you wanted to see me." She said.

Gabriel Astruc glanced up at her. "Yes, my dear." He said, tossing the photographs aside. "Do you know who I am?"

"Maître Clunet told me you're a booking agent."

"Indeed. I brought the Ballets Russes de Monte Carlo to France." He said, gesturing to a photograph on the wall.

Margaretha glanced at the picture of the ballet dancers, then back at Astruc. "You want me for a ballet?"

"Not exactly. I asked you in here because I saw your act last night at Madame Kiréesky's."

"I take it then you liked what you saw..."

"I'm going to be blunt, my dear - your skill is *not* in your dance movements..."

"It's not?"

"No. It's in your sex appeal."

He studied her reaction. Margaretha just looked at him and smiled.

"But *you* already know that." He said with a wry grin. "Excellent."

Astruc began pacing the office floor as he thought.

"Now, we need to give you a new name..."

"What do you mean?"

"Lady McLeod? Come on, that sounds like a common dance-hall girl. We need something with a little pizazz!"

"I've been using the name Mata Hari at a couple of performances" Margaretha said, "But I don't know..."

Margaretha could almost see the wheels turning in his head as he walked about the office, puffing on the cigar.

Gabriel Astruc

"All things Oriental *are* the rage right now." He said, thinking out loud. "That American gal, what's her name..." He snaped his fingers "...Isadora Duncan - she's making a name for herself by just going barefoot in a leg-baring toga!"

"Then you like it?"

"I like it. Mata Hari..." Astruc said, picturing the name on a poster. "And that dance you perform - does it have a name?"

"Not really. It's based on a dance called Gandrung - a traditional dance in Java - usually performed all night."

"I've heard of it. It was originally danced to show love and dedication to Dewi Sri, the goddess of rice and fertility, I believe. No matter –

yours is a dance that combines raw eroticism with a thin veneer of religiosity - it's perfect!"

Margaretha raised her eyebrows and smiled.

"And correct me if I am wrong," he said, draping his arm over her shoulder, "but don't these dancers usually pick partners from the audience who donate money to them in appreciation?"

"They do."

"Then all we need to do is get you into a better costume."

Margaretha nodded. "I've been working on putting one together from Maître Clunet's fine collection of Javanese garments."

"Excellent." Astruc said, picking up his telephone. "Now, with your permission, I'm going to book you to an engagement at the Olympia Theater on the Boulevard des Capucines."

"Yes - of course!" She said excitedly. "That's the best theater in Paris!"

Margaretha anxiously stood aside while he booked the engagement over the phone. Hanging up, Astruc looked at her and smiled.

"You'll finish out the August 20 program - after a group of Arabian dancers, a juggler, Leo and his Infernal Violin, an acrobatic act, as well as some cinematographic projections."

"After?"

"Think about it, my dear - If you went on first, by the time Leo and his violin appeared, the place would be empty."

"And my pay?"

"Ten thousand francs - of which I get ten percent - that's the standard deal."

A broad smile stretched across her face.

"I promise," She smiled, "you will *not* be disappointed."

August 20, 1905

BACKSTAGE AT THE Olympia Theater, Astruc nervously looked over Margaretha, now fully decked out in her homemade costume — transparent veils over a metallic brassiere, and a headpiece adorned with fake jewels.

"Now, remember, as you dance, you take this off piece by piece, working yourself up to a fever pitch. Then, at the climactic moment, you prostrate yourself all but naked at the feet of the idol on stage."

Margaretha smiled, looking him in the eye.

"The performance was a complete success." She told Sister Leonide. "The next day, my act was reviewed in *La Presse*. They wrote: "one would need special words, new words, to explain the tender and charming art of Mata Hari! Maybe one could simply say that this woman is rhythm, thus, to indicate, as closely as possible, the poetry which emanates from this magnificently supple and beautiful body."

Margaretha blushed. "I'm afraid I had spent far more money than I made during those first six months. Now that I was receiving a large and steady salary, a Paris jeweler caught up with me and had my paycheck attached for my unpaid bill."

"I couldn't have been for that much..." The Sister said.

"That's what I thought. But it totaled over twelve thousand francs."

Sister Leonide's eyes grew wide. Margaretha shrugged. "What can I say?"

"And they paid you this for your exquisite dancing?"

Margaretha laughed. "Of course not. I never could dance very well. They paid me that because I was the first woman who dared to show myself naked to the public." See looked directly at the nun. "I am not naïve, Sister Leonide. With every veil I threw off, my success rose. Pretending to consider my dances to be very artistic and full of character, thus praising my art, they actually came to see nudity." "In my dancing one forgets the woman in me, so that when I offer everything and finally myself to the god—which is symbolized by the loosening of my loincloth, the last piece of clothing I have on—and stand there - albeit for only a second - entirely naked, I have never yet evoked any feeling but the interest in the mood that is expressed by my dancing."

"Then one day I got a call from Maître Clunet. Even though we no longer slept together, I had retained him as my lawyer..."

88

MARGARETHA SAT AT the table of the outdoor café that warm August morning, sipping her tea. Clunet quietly sat to one side - sitting across from her was another lawyer, one Mr. Heijmans.

"Okay," She said to Heijmans, "I am here. What is it that is so important?"

"As you know, your husband wants a divorce..."

"Going to be a beautiful day – isn't it?" She said, deliberately changing the subject.

"Listen to me, damn it!" He said, striking the table with his fist.

Margaretha looked at him – then took another sip of tea.

"I came here to Paris from Amsterdam a week ago!" Heijmans said forcefully.

"I've met and talked to you nearly every day for the past week But every time the divorce is brought up, you change the subject!"

"That's because he need's *her* consent to do so, Mr. Heijmans." Clunet told him.

"Well...?" He asked, turning to Margaretha.

"At this time, I have not the slightest inclination to give it."

Mr. Heijmans sat back in his chair – and sighed. "Okay." He said, digging into his briefcase. "I'm through being subtle."

Heijmans pulled out a nude 8x10 photograph of her as Mata Hari and tossed it in front of her.

"Where did you get this?!" Margaretha asked angrily.

"That photograph," he explained, "was purchased here in Paris and sent to your husband by an anonymous friend."

"But this was never meant for sale! It was taken privately for a friend of mine!"

"That might well be the case." Mr. Heijmans said. "But a stern judge in Holland might be of the opinion that an *honorable* woman and mother would not have herself photographed in the nude – even for a friend."

Margaretha flipped the photograph back to Heijmans.

"Go to hell."

"Think of your daughter, Margaretha. Do you *really* want *her* to be mixed up in a public scandal?"

She leveled her gaze at him.

"You're not leaving me with much of a choice, are you?"

"Only the logical one." He pushed the divorce papers in front of her. "Sign – and the picture is yours."

"Why I ever answered that damn advertisement I'll never know." She said, signing it.

Looking the paper over, Heijmans then tucked it into his briefcase and stood up.

"It was a pleasure doing business with you." He said, tossing the nude photograph onto the table.

"Get out." She said, ripping the photograph in half. "And don't come back."

Chapter 9

"Her face makes a strange, foreign, impression"

❖ ❖ ❖

January 1906

MY PERFORMANCES AT the Olympia Theater proved a complete success. Knowing a good thing when he saw it, Gabriel Astruc officially signed me on as a client after the first night and actively promoted my career from then on."

"Four months before my divorce I left for a two-week engagement dancing at the Central Kursaal in Madrid, Spain. Clunet even provided me with a letter to a friend of his in the Spanish capitol, the French ambassador, Jules Cambon. Not wanting to create more fuel for my husband's lawyer, and not knowing some nude photos of me were already being made into picture post cards in Paris, Clunet suggested I dance in a body stocking."

"And how were you received in Spain?"

"The Spanish press called my dances 'discreetly voluptuous.' But they regretted that I danced in tights." She glanced at the Sister. "And to tell the truth – so did I."

In her dressing room at the Central Kursaal in Madrid, Margaretha was cleaning up after a performance when a knock came at her door.

In bodystocking - 1906

Answering the knock, the stage manager handed Margaretha a letter then walked away. Opening the envelope, she sees it is from Astruc.

"I take pleasure in informing you that I have just signed a contract with my friend Raoul Gunsbourg, the director of the Opera in Monte Carlo, for Mata Hari to appear there in the ballet of Massenet's *Le Roi de Lahore*. The ballet is being sponsored by Prince Albert of Monaco, and promises to be an outstanding season."

"This was the chance I'd been waiting for!"

"I don't understand. It sounds as though you were quite successful..."

"I was - but up until this point I appeared only in oriental dances of my own invention. This was serious theater. Now I could prove to my critics I could really dance - not just move and pose."

"And what did you do?"

"I immediately replied to the letter, asking Astruc to please send me the score of the opera."

February 17, 1906

92

Sitting in his private box in the theater, the composer of the opera, Massenet, watched in fascination as Margaretha danced the ballet of the opera's third act in the company of the famous Mademoiselle Zambeli. When the curtain came down the audience erupted into applause. Massenet, clapping his hands furiously, jumped to his feet, entirely won over by her.

As Margaretha made her way to her dressing room backstage, she was handed a huge bouquet of flowers by a delivery man.

"From Puccini." The man told her. "To congratulate you on your success."

Margaretha sniffed the flowers and smiled.

"The press called me "a seductive star" bringing to the ballet "the troubling charm of my strange dances." She sighed. "I've never been one to let an opportunity pass, so I began pestering Massenet to compose an opera exclusively for me."

"Well?"

"At first, he seemed interested, but... I pursued the idea for several years – until I finally realized it was never going to come about."

❖   ❖   ❖

April 26, 1906

ADAM ZELLE SAT at the breakfast table of his home at Da Costakade 65 in Amsterdam, reading the newspaper. Turning the page, he came to an article extolling the sensational new internationally acclaimed dancer, Mata Hari, and photograph of his daughter in costume.

His wife since 1893, Susanna Catharina ten Hoove entered the room to find Adam lost in thought.

"Is everything all right?" She asked.

"Did you see this article?" He asked.

"About that Asian lady who likes to dance around naked? Yes, I have. She's been in the news for the last month."

"Well, that "lady" is my daughter, Margaretha."

"Really?!" She glanced at the photograph. "You don't seem very surprised..."

"Look at this..." he said, flicking the newspaper with his fingers. "Here I am, the father of a famous woman – a "lady" who is an acclaimed dancer – living like a pauper."

"We may not be wealthy, but your job as a traveling salesman pays the rent and keeps food on the table."

"But there isn't money enough for much else, is there? I'm tired of living like this – I yearn for the luxuries I once had during Margaretha's youth."

"Just what are you thinking?"

"I was wondering if I can tap into Margaretha's growing fame as Mata Hari..." He glanced at Susanna. "I took some notes letters and papers to an Amsterdam book publisher last week and asked him to arrange the material into a biography of her."

"Well?" She asked.

"He said the subject looked interesting – until the man met up with McLeod, her ex-husband. I never liked him. The publisher said McLeod completely contradicted my story – not to mention those stories Margaretha is telling the journalists. He told me yesterday he's abandoning the project."

"So, seek out another publisher." Susanna told him. There a dozens of them here in Amsterdam."

Adam raised his eyebrows.

August 1906

MATA HARI TOOK BERLIN by storm that summer. So much so, she even managed to beguile a lieutenant in the Second Company of the 11th Westphalian Hussars Regiment. Herr Alfred Kiepert was the Duke of Cumberland, and cousin of English King George V (who had sided with Germany and married his son to the Kaiser's daughter, and Crown Prince Wilhelm.). A rich landowner whose estate was just outside the city, Kiepert, although married to a Hungarian Beauty, he now wanted Margaretha as his mistress. To make sure she would be available to him at a moment's notice he put her up in an apartment at number 39 in the Nachodstrasse, within walking distance of the Kurfürstendamm, the main artery of Berlin.

While there she wrote a letter from Berlin to her manager and agent, Gabriel Astruc in Paris.

"I have just received an offer from London to appear in a pantomime, which pleases me enormously. But I would much rather do it in Monte Carlo where I have had such a great success."

Margaretha, as Mata Hari, was hot. And it seemed all of Europe wanted her

December 1906

Margaretha was walking down a busy Paris street when she paused at a window display in a bookstore. There on display was the 266 page book *The Life of Mata Hari - the Biography of My Daughter and My Grievances Against Her Former Husband* - by Adam Zelle.

Margaretha let out a mournful sigh – then went into the store and purchased a copy.

Two days later a frustrated Margaretha paced the offices of Maître Clunet as he looked over the book.

"Where did you find this?" Clunet asked.

"Find it? It's in the window of every bookstore in Paris! You can't walk down the street without it staring at you in the face."

"It says here you're actually the descendant of dukes, kings, and a scattering of lesser noblemen. Is that true?"

She gave him a tired look. "Of course not."

"So, you're not 76 years old?"

96

Margretha laughed. "I'm 28. He also claims the first half of the book was written by me – I supposedly sent it to him from the United States of America."

"Since when were you in the United States?"

"It must have been while on vacation with one of those dukes."

"You know, the little I've read alone constitutes a nice case for libel."

She waved the suggestion off. "He isn't worth the trouble. I just wish I knew where all this came from..."

"I talked to a publisher friend of mine in Amsterdam yesterday. He said the pages were actually penned by two female ghost writers whose expertise is in romance novels. They went to your father and asked if he would allow them to use his name. He agreed, and gave them your photographs and they wrote the book. Your father gave it the title."

"It's a horrible book!" She said. "I just can't figure out why he did it..."

"Money." Clunet said, setting the book aside. "It is always money. But I wouldn't worry about it. The general public will quickly see through the nonsense and lose interest."

Margaretha nodded. Clunet then pulled out a package of Mata Hari Cigarettes and lit one up. Incredulous, Margaretha picked up the package.

"What's this?" she asked.

"This is what happens when you don't copyright the name. With the attention on all things Mata Hari for the time being a Dutch cigarette manufacturer saw his chance to cash in. With nothing to stop him, he put Mata Hari Cigarettes out on the market."

"Are they any good?" She asked.

"To quote their advertising, they are "the newest Indian cigarette, which will be satisfying to the most refined taste, made from the best Sumatra and choice Turkish tobacco."

"How much?"

"One hundred Mata Hari's, exclusively in a Russian blend, mind you considered to be very refined, are available in both yellow and white for one guilder and twenty-five cents."

97

"If you see an ad for the cigarettes in a newspaper," Margaretha told him, "Save it for me."

"Okay – but why?"

"I want to cut it out and paste it into my scrap book." She gathered herself together. "Well, I have to be off. I don't want to miss my train."

"Where are you going?"

"On December 14, 1906, I am scheduled to appear again at the

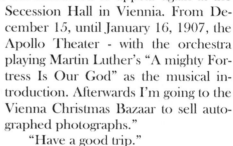

Secession Hall in Viennia. From December 15, until January 16, 1907, the Apollo Theater - with the orchestra playing Martin Luther's "A mighty Fortress Is Our God" as the musical introduction. Afterwards I'm going to the Vienna Christmas Bazaar to sell autographed photographs."

"Have a good trip."

"My fans were somewhat disappointed when I came dressed like everyone else."

"Oh? Why is that?"

"They hoped I was going to appear in costume." She laughed. "Or perhaps without it."

"Even so, the reviewers said I "quickly delighted the crowd" with my "slender, shapely appearance." I was even told I looked as adorable with my clothes on, as off."

"Slender and tall." One journalist wrote, "with the flexible grace of a wild animal, and with blue-black hair surrounding the small face that makes a strange, foreign impression.

"I pasted all of my reviews, good, bad, or indifferent, into my scrap books."

Chapter 10

"I find myself in rather difficult circumstances..."

❖   ❖   ❖

February 1907

IT WAS A COLD and miserable Wednesday in Viennia when Margaretha, on the arm of Lieutenant Kiepert, stepped aboard the steamer *Schleswig* for the five-day journey to Egypt. Now openly Kiepert's mistress, the two spent the next two months crisscrossing the land of the pharaohs, visiting the night clubs and parlors in Alexandria and Cairo where she hoped to discover some different classical dances for her act. But she soon became dismayed.

"Everything that is lovely has disappeared," She wrote to Astruc from the old Hotel Bristol in Rome, "and the dances that are left are insignificant and not graceful."

"I understand you are to produce the first Paris performance of *Salome* by Richard Strauss at the Châtelet Theater on May 10. I would like nothing better than to dance in that opera.

"The music by Strauss is powerful," She wrote. "And I would love to create and interpret the meaning of the dance – which is usually the weak point of an opera. A badly executed dance cuts all effect.

"I will be back at my apartment at 39 Nachodstrasse in Berlin within a few days."

"I've enclosed a letter to Strauss for you to forward."

Margaretha Zelle

As Margaretha and Kiepert finally departed Rome at the end of March, Astruc sat at the desk in his office reading her letter. Finishing, he laid it aside, picking up the letter for Strauss. He contemplated for a moment, then dropped it into a filing cabinet, slid the drawer shut, and forgot about it. For reasons unknown, she would never dance in his production of the opera.

December 1907

MARGARETHA RETURNED to Paris, disillusioned by her eight months abroad, only to find an untold number of shapely women now imitating her act in the theaters and cabarets.

"You have only yourself to blame." Gabriel told her one afternoon in his office. "Without realizing it, you have shown other young women that a naked, well-shaped female can find easy employment in a Paris music hall."

"I assure you, that was not my intent."

"And you have to take into consideration your older body..."

"What? I'm only 33..."

"I know – and you're still very attractive. But be realistic - you've borne two children. How long do you think a body like that will maintain the same appeal as those lithe younger girls?"

"Maybe I should go in a totally new direction, you know, like dancing in a dress with a long train."

"I'd hold off doing that – at least until the end of the new year." He dug into his filing cabinet and pulled out her file. "I've got you booked up for one benefit after another, all the way through September of 1908, including one for the Japanese ambassador, Baron Kurino. The bookings wind up on October 4, 1908, where you'll appear at the

Grand Prix d'Automne at Longchamps. Make sure you wear that magnificent velvet dress of yours."

"I eventually grew tired of doing benefit performances." She told Sister Leonide. "So, I posed for an oil painting by Paul Frantz-Namur sometime during 1909. Other than this, I stayed out of the limelight." And why not? Lieutenant Kiepert, had set me up in Berlin and I received the protection of the richest strangers, and I did not lack the skill to profit from that, let me assure you."

"Then, in March of 1909, Kiepert returned to his wife. But he left me comfortable with a gift of three hundred thousand marks, which I promptly deposited in the private bank of Xavier Rousseau."

"Now free of attachments I played the field. One night I would dine with Count A, the next with Duke B, and if I did not have to dance, the next day I took a trip with Marquis C. I avoided serious liaisons, turning down several offered wedding rings – all because of what had happened with my ex-husband."

"But along the way I did become the mistress of several – Jules Cambon, French ambassador in Madrid, for one, and then the banker, Rousseau."

January 1910

MONTE CARLO. The play was called *Antar*, set in Arabia and written by a French-Algerian named Chekri-Ganem. Margaretha, now 34, appeared as Cleopatra, performing a ballet danced by a single person in the third act. She was perfect for the part, giving "a beautiful performance that was successively smiling, mystical, and impressive."

It was the play's director, Monsieur Carlo Antoine, who brought Margaretha to Monte Carlo. But when he brought *Antar* back to his own theater in Paris, her head swelled with the accolades and she became difficult once rehearsals started. Having become the mistress of the married banker and stockbroker, Xavier Rousseau, who was only three years older than herself, she began showing up late, her "proud character" eventually making theater life for the other actors impossible.

Finally having enough of her antics, Monsieur Antoine fired her. From February of 1910 to December of 1911, Margaretha, and subsequently Mata Hari, virtually disappeared from the public record, during which time she sued Antoine for breach of contract, demanding three-thousand francs for her salary and five-thousand francs damages.

She won, and was paid the three-thousand francs – but nothing else. Not needing the money, she wasn't too concerned – he'd pay up sooner or later.

June 1910

XAVIER ROUSSEAU, very good looking, "honest and serious," had met Margaretha, at the time living in a hotel in Paris, at a soiree where his son, who was a musician, played. The love affair quickly turned into one of her greatest passions and he rented the Château de la Dorée in Esvres, near Tours, owned by the widowed Comtesse de la Taille-Trétinville.

Margaretha and Monsieur Rousseau arrived at the Château, bringing her four horses and a carriage with them. The butler, an overly serious and conservative man named Delacôte, stood stiff and proper in his crisp uniform in front of the rest of the staff lined up in the driveway, ready to greet the new residents.

"Delacôte," said Rousseau as he stepped from the carriage, "This is Madame van Zellen. She's the widow of the English Lord MacDonald, a former governor general of the Indies. We have recently wed. You may call her Mrs. Rousseau."

Delacôte nodded. "Mademoiselle." He said to her, bowing slightly.

Entering the front doors of the massive building, Margaretha was a little surprised by all the activity. Workmen busily went to and fro and all sorts of industry, such as sawing and hammering filled the air. She gave Xavier a questioning glance.

"When I rented the mansion," he explained, "I only saw the beautiful large front room. I had no idea the house had neither bathrooms,

102

indoor plumbing of any kind, electricity or gas. So, I've hired workers, at considerable expense mind you, to bring the Château into the 20th century. I'll pay for your deluxe accommodations in a hotel in Paris, until the chateau is ready to inhabit next week."

Margaretha turned to Delacôte, who had followed them indoors, discreetly staying a few paces behind them.

"Please inform the stableman that Monsieur Rousseau and I will be going riding together in the mornings along the Bois de Boulogne, and that I would like the two horses, Rajah, and Son of Upas, saddled and ready for us."

"Yes ma'am."

"I can see it now," Xavier said, picturing her riding, "Your thick hair covered with either a *chapeau melon* or a top hat, you'll cut a beautiful figure on the lanes of the Bois. Those who see you pass by on one of your magnificent horses, will be impressed by the grace, nobleness, and beauty of your aristocratic *cavaliere*. And no one will imagine that this admirable amazon is none but Mata Hari, the holy dancer!"

"Only you." She said, giggling. "Oh, and my friend, Anna Lintjens, of course. She will be arriving next week."

"Delacôte," Xavier said, "Tell the coachman that I will be arriving at the Tours train station on Friday evenings. I expect the carriage there to meet me. The coachman will return me back to Tours early on Monday morning. Is that clear?"

"As you wish, Monsieur."

But almost the moment Xavier left for Paris that first Friday after they moved in, Margaretha found herself at loggerheads with the existing staff. The first incident took place the next morning.

Margaretha appeared in the dining room at 9:30 a.m. passing some of the staff who gave her dirty looks.

"I don't understand." Margaretha told Anna as she sat down at the table. "Everyone seems so cross."

Delacôte, leading a young girl from the kitchen, stepped up to Margaretha's table.

"Madame," he said with the utmost seriousness, "it is my duty to report that your personal maid, Pauline, was making coffee for the early staff before you arose. What disciplinary action do you want me to take?"

"Disciplinary action?" Margaretha scoffed. "She was only making coffee while I slept in. Wait – that's not *your* job – is it?"

"Of course not. "But she knows one of the rules of the household is that none of the staff can eat before her ladyship."

"But I no longer have an early large breakfast."

Delacôte became irate. "Madame. The Comtesse de la Taille-Trétinville always insisted upon staff maintaining strict dress codes and following the letter of her demands."

"Well, you're not catering to that snob at the moment, are you?" She looked at Pauline. "Dear, if the staff wants coffee and I'm still asleep – go right ahead and make it."

Delacôte stiffened up - now seeing Margaretha as beneath him. From then on, during every long, five-day interval between Monsieur Rousseau visits, the butler treated Margaretha with little more than contempt.

One morning, a sixteen-year-old boy, a relative of Comtesse de la Taille-Trétinville, rode up to the Château on horseback where Margaretha sat with Anna outside on the terrace drinking their breakfast coffee.

"I've just ridden all the way nonstop from Paris!" He said proudly, dismounting. "To bring Madame van Zellen this letter."

"So, you think that quite an accomplishment, do you?" She asked, taking the letter, glancing at it and setting it aside.

"I do." He said, breaking out in a broad smile.

Margaretha suddenly jumped into the horse's saddle and with both Anna and the boy watching in amazement, rode up and down the entire outer staircase of the Château.

She then returned to where the astonished boy stood. "When you can do *that*," she told him, "You can say you know how to ride."

She then slid out of the saddle, handed the reins back to him, and rejoined Anna at the terrace table.

IT WASN'T LONG before word of "Madame van Zellen's" antics and thorough disregard for the strict rules of etiquette leaked back to the real Madame Rousseau, who remained living in Paris the entire time, perfectly aware of everything her husband was doing.

Xavier's mother, who lived in Buzançais and was simply referred to as Old Madame Rousseau by the family, sat across from her step-daughter in the Livingroom of her large home in Paris, the two talking over the situation with Xavier and Margaretha.

"I'm told they, at least, have separate bedrooms..." The wife said between sips of tea.

"Surely you can't believe separate bedrooms manage to poise much of a barrier between two people who want to see each other." Old Madame Rousseau commented.

"Of course not. But if my information is correct, she sleeps on a mauve-colored canopy bed on a raised platform. You have to walk up a few steps to get to it. I'll bet Xavier's tripped over that in the dark a time or two."

"The Comtesse de la Taille-Trétinville tells me that van Zellen has lived at the Château for but a month," Old Madame Rousseau told her, "And already the entire staff has been replaced by new help. The butler told her: "We are very glad to leave the employ of M. Rousseau and his mistress, for the situation as La Dorée at this moment is deplorable." The mother glanced at the wife. "I warned you he was a skirt-chaser."

"So, I guess I shouldn't have been surprised when he took Mar-garetha as his mistress." Madame Rousseau stated.

"Maybe as his mother, I can persuade this "Madame van Zellen" to give up my son. I'll visit the Château when he comes back to Paris and she what kind of woman she really is."

August 1911

MUCH TO THE chagrin of the wife, the moment Old Mad-ame Rousseau met Margaretha, she was charmed by her and they became fast friends.

When the mother finally departed six months later, she was calling Margaretha "Madame Rousseau" and left her still in charge of the Château.

"How much do you know about my son?" Old Madame Rousseau asked Margaretha just before leaving.

"Only that he is the Director-General of his own bank. I deposited Three hundred thousand marks into it myself."

"My dear, Xavier started his private bank less than three years ago. So far, he's been forced to put up 125,000 francs of his own money to keep it operating."

"What are you saying?"

"Heed my advice." Old Madame Rousseau warned Margaretha. "My Xavier may be a charming man – but unlike his father, he does *not* have a head for business. Without your timely deposit, his bank would most likely be in serious trouble. If I were you, I would not be so reliant on him. Be smart - obtain a residence of your own."

"So, I did." She told Sister Leonide. "Shortly after his mother left I rented an extremely charming house just outside Paris proper, situated at 11 Rue Windsor in the suburb of Neuilly-sur-Seine."

Margaretha walked through the empty structure built in the Normandy style around 1860. She marveled at the plastered walls of the house and how they were crisscrossed with wooden beams. While the second floor was composed of four bedrooms off a central hall, the ground floor had only two fairly large rooms, one of which had an open fireplace, and both of which looked out on the garden that had a gate with double doors that opened onto a small courtyard with stables on the far side.

"So here you are..." Xavier said, walking into the room and looking it over. "It seems overly Spartan for one of your taste."

"I like it – I now have a chance to start anew."

"Oh yes," He said as an afterthought, "the mailman handed me this on the way in."

Taking the small package from him, she looked it over and sighed.

"Is something wrong?" he asked.

"No – not really." She said. "It's just – well, I purchased a gold watch and had Anna mail it to my 13-year-old daughter in Amsterdam a few weeks ago. Now, here it is - returned unopen. It says refused right here - in John's handwriting. I'll bet he did it without even letting Non know about it."

Unsure what to say, Xavier changed the subject.

"I see the stables of your new home already house your four thoroughbreds..."

"Yes - I brought with me from the Château. Now that they are here, I was planning to go into Paris and purchase the furniture I need for myself."

"Don't bother." He told her. "I am friends with the owner of the largest furniture broker in the city. Nothing would make me happier than to fill the house with all new furniture for you."

"Why thank you, Xavier." She said, giving him a kiss. "I accept."

"I had been at new house in Neuilly-sur-Seine less than two months, when, on a cold and rainy evening, Xavier visited me, hat in hand, his gaze fixed upon the floor. My fears concerning him suddenly came true..."

"I have made... poor investments...for the bank" Xavier told her tearfully, his pitiful figure wilting in the rain. "I am ruined."

"Then I am withdrawing my money from your bank immediately." She told him. "I believe I still have about two hundred and eighty-five thousand marks in my account. Please have a cashier's check made out for the full amount."

Standing in the pouring rain, his lip quivering, Xavier just looked at her with a pained expression on his face.

"What is it?!" She demanded, suspecting he wasn't telling her the whole truth. "Tell me!"

"Your money –it was the bank's money."

"Are you telling me... My money - is that how you paid for the Château?!"

107

"I am... so ashamed - so sorry."

"Now it all makes sense!" She said, snatching a handful of opened letters from her table. "These overdue notices I've been receiving from the furniture company! Demanding their money or threatening to reclaim the furniture! You never paid them a penny – did you?!"

He shook his head without saying a word.

"And you've been using *my* money to cover the bank's losses?! And now you say you are *bankrupt* after draining my account?!"

"Not just yours..."

"All of them?!" Margaretha was stunned. "Everyone who invested with you?!"

Thunder rumbled in the sky as he meekly nodded his head. The pouring rain increased as if it were an extension of the tears welling in Margaretha's eyes.

"Get out!" She ordered, feeling stupid for allowing herself to be taken such total advantage of. "Get out of my house – and out of my life!"

Margaretha collapsed to the floor sobbing as Anna, who'd been listening from an adjoining room, stepped in and confronted Xavier.

"Go back home to your wife!" Anna ordered Xavier, slamming the front door closed in his face. She then knelt down and turned her attention to Margaretha.

An hour later, in the pouring rain, Xavier stood at the end of the driveway of a large mansion in Paris. He watched as it was illuminated by a flash of lightning and marveled at how he seemed so small against the backdrop of the immense black clouds and pouring rain. As the rain increased, he shuffled down the driveway towards the house.

Inside the mansion, the real Madame Rousseau sat curled up on a couch reading, when her butler, Francois, entered the room.

"Who is at the front door?" She asked Francois.

"Your husband. He insists on seeing you, Madame." The butler told her. "Do you want me to call the police?"

"No - I'll handle this, Francois."

"Very well, madame."

Approaching the open door, she looked out to see Xavier standing on the front steps in the cold rain. Seeing her, he removed his hat and looked at the ground. She looked him over as Francois receded into the interior shadows.

"Well?" She asked, Xavier. "What have you got to say for yourself?"

"I beg of you," he pleaded, "I... I am ruined."

She studied the poor, broken figure of a man for a few moments then sighed. "You look like a wet dog. If you had one, your tail would be between your legs."

Xavier stood silently, not raising his head as the pouring rain drained from his coat and pooled in the brick covered streets around him.

She sighed again - then stepped aside the wide-open front door. Xavier entered and shuffled past her like a wounded animal.

"You have taken him back?" Francois asked, taking the front door as Madame followed her husband up the interior stairway.

"Of course." She said. "What other choice do I have?"

Francois shook his head, closing the door behind them, shutting out the prying eyes of the world.

Chapter 11

"I had a lifestyle to maintain..."

❖   ❖   ❖

October 1911

G ABRIEL ASTRUC SAT in his office, going through his paperwork when his phone rang. Without even looking at the ringing instrument, he casually reached over and picked up the receiver.

"Astruc Agency." He stated matter of factly.

"Gabriel? This is Margaretha Zelle..."

Smiling, he leaned back in his chair. "My dear Mata Hari. What has it been – two years?"

"I wish this were a casual call – but I am desperate for money. Is there anyplace you can book me?"

"You are in luck. The woman who was to play Venus in Marenco's *Bacco e Gambrinus* at La Scala, the opera house in Milan, has fallen ill – well, actually she is pregnant and starting to show. She can no longer hide the fact with tights. They have asked me to find a replacement."

"You've found her. Go ahead and book me for the season."

"Leon Bakst, the stage designer, has the decorative power of the dance group. He's assigned to create some of Venus' costumes."

"I do not need Bakst. I made my own costume. Before leaving for Milan, I am having some photographs made of me as Venus. You can then send them to the newspapers abroad."

"I was 36. I went on to dance two ballets at La Scala during the 1911-1912 season. My success in Milan finally proved that I'd been indisputably accepted as a professional dancer. At the season's opening I even met Preobrajenska..."

"The famous ballerina?"

Margaretha nodded. "She gave me some precious advice."

"With my success at La Scala, Grabriel sought to get me accepted into the Diaghilev Ballet Group..."

"The premier Russian ballet?"

Margaretha nodded.

"He worked out the details of a contract. I signed my copy in Milan, which I sent back to Grabriel in Paris. Now all he had to do was get Diaghilev to sign it."

"While we waited for his signature, I went on to dance *The Princess and the Magic Flower* in the fifth act of in Gluck's opera *Armida*. On January 4, 1912, I appeared as Venus again, this time in *Bacchus and Gambrinus*. I played Venus with my own hair, therefore dark. They were astonished."

"The next day the Italian newspaper, *Lombardia* stated my movements were "executed in perfect harmony, worthy of our admiration.""

111

"Gabriel and his business partner, Raoul Gunsbourg, then brought *Les Ballets* from Monte Carlo to France, and he prepared for me to dance with them."

"Working all these shows - was it out of demand – or necessity?"

"Necessity. Money was always a problem after Xavier Rousseau squandered my private fortune. Why do you think I had to return to the theater?" She asked Sister Leonide.

"Returning home in Neuilly on February 8, 1912, I found I was still

being dunned for the cost of the furniture Rousseau so "generously" provided - along with a mountain of unpaid bills for the upkeep of the house and stables."

Sister Leonide shook her head.

"Don't misunderstand - I took in a great deal of money – three thousand francs a month for my role as Venus, and likewise in Milan – but I spent a great deal, too."

"But why, dear?"

"I had a lifestyle to maintain, after all." She sighed. "I again turned to Gabriel for financial help..."

Margaretha paced Gabriel's office as her manager, sitting at his desk leaned back in his chair and watched.

"I wonder if you know anyone," She asked as she walked back and forth, "who would be interested in the protection of artists?"

"I'm sorry." He said. "What?"

"You know - like a capitalist who would like to make an investment."

"Margaretha – I know you've been going to bed with certain men to get a little cash... are you asking me to be your pimp?"

She turned and gave him an annoyed look. "Of course not. It's just that I find myself in rather difficult circumstances at the moment."

"How difficult?"

"I need thirty thousand francs immediately – or all the furniture in my home will be repossessed. I must get out of this unpleasant situation! Tranquility of mind is so necessary to my art - it would really be a pity to cut such a future short!"

"So, in essence, you're seeking a loan." She nodded. "What have you got as a guarantee?"

"I offer everything I have in my home, including my horses and carriages. All monies will be paid back within two or three years out of the fees you will be able to get me."

She glanced at Sister Léonide. "I never did find anyone willing to shower any financial gifts upon me. But that didn't stop me from living as if I had an ample supply of funds on my part."

"So, what did you do?"

"Strapped for money, for the next month I danced for low pay in musical comedies in Paris."

"It wasn't until mid-March that the preliminary talks with Diaghilev, you know, about joining the ballet, had reached the point where he deemed it necessary to meet me in person."

March 15, 1912

Margaretha, once again in Garbiel's office, stormed about the room as Astruc sat behind his desk, watching her with a wary eye.

"He wants me to work first - and only then will he *perhaps* sign a contract?!" She threw up her hands. "But I am an accomplished artist!" She shouted at her agent. "Why should I have to show him what I am capable of?"

"What can I say? That's what he told me."

"But my dancing is known all over Europe..."

"Listen, he simply refuses to sign a contract with you, sight unseen. Diaghilev wants to judge your dancing for himself - before giving you the lead in his Dance of the Goddess."

Margaretha paused herself and looked at Gabriel. "But..." She stammered. "It's just that it's a requirement I've never before come up against."

"And I have more potentially bad news for you."

Her eyes rolled up to look at him – asking the question.

"Leon Bakst has been hired to be Diaghilev's costume designer. This time there is no option – he designs the costumes – period." He looked her in the eye. "And the word is He's still smarting from your rejection."

March 21, 1912

Margaretha answered the door to her hotel room in Monte Carlo to find Bakst standing there, a tape measure slung around his neck, hanging over his clothes like a loose scarf.

"Yes?' She asked.

"I'm Leon Bakst." He said, walking into the room uninvited. "I'm here to see what kind of body I am going to dress."

He looked her over as she closed the door. "Please undress completely."

"For the likes of you? I will not."

"Are you saying you would rather we do this on the stage of Beausoleil, where all stagehands can freely pass by?"

She gave him a dirty look. "Fine."

"What is your age?" he asked, looking her over as she began to undress.

"I'm 36 going on 37."

"How long have you been dancing?"

"Six or seven years."

"29 is rather late in life to begin a career in ballet. But I have to admit, you look great for a woman who's given birth to two kids – but..."

"But what?"

"You started your career at an age when others begin to think of their retirement from the profession."

"So?"

"About performing with the Ballet Russe – I'm afraid I'm going to advise Diaghilev that you're not fit for the part."

She narrowed her eyes at him as she slipped on her dressing gown. "You're just angry I didn't use you in Milian!"

"Perhaps – but that doesn't change the fact that your figure is much too matronly!"

"How dare you!"

"You forget I also am in this business. I know all about what happened when you danced the role of Cleopatra in *Antar*."

"Oh? What about it?"

"When the opera moved to the Odeon in Paris, Andre Antoine, the director, fired you for putting on too much weight!"

"And, I sued for breach of contract - and won!"

Bakst laughed. "Knowing Andre, I'd be surprised if you've collected so much as a penny from him."

A knock came at her hotel door. Opening it, she was handed a telegram by a bellboy. She stepped back to let Bakst leave her room. Without a word the costume designer brushed passed her and disappeared down the hallway. Handing the bellboy a tip, she closed the door and opened the telegram. It read:

"I have been rehearsing late and am sorry not to have been able to work on the dance of the Goddess. Diaghilev."

In disbelief, she sighed then plopped back against a wall, dropping her arms.

"So, I've traveled to Monte Carlo to meet with him – for nothing."

115

She looked at herself in the full-length mirror on the wall across from her. For the first time she realized age was beginning to catch up with her. While by no means fat, she no longer possessed the lithe, slim body of her youth. A single tear trickled down her cheek.

June 21, 1912

MARGARETHA STOOD quietly at the window of Gabreil Astruc's office in Paris – her calm demeanor a complete contrast to her former visits. He just watched and listened.

"I must tell you that the story of the Ballet Russe has put me in a most awkward position."

"Oh? Why is that?"

She turned from the window and looked at him. "Because I talked too much about it. I admit I may have spread a few stories about my upcoming debut with the prestigious opera..."

"And now you're experiencing the unhappy repercussions of your premature statements. Is that it?"

She nodded. "My career has gone into a serious decline... Although I continue to appear in public wearing the latest Paris fashion, attended the Auteuil races on the occasion of the running of the Grand Prix at Easter, was photographed riding Son of Upas, and even made an appearance at the Grand Steeple Chase with a smiling face and the bravado of a successful artist – in truth, my life at this point has become little more than a façade."

"So, now you're hounding me to get you more work." She nodded. "I'm afraid, for now your act will only be seen in society circles and select social events."

"I am perfectly willing to go elsewhere." She told him. "Will you please try London and the United States if Vienna does not succeed? But that would amaze me – for it is there that I have been acclaimed the most."

"I'm sorry, Margaretha." He said, standing and stepping to the front of his desk. "Right now, I'm busy with a number of other clients and projects in development. I just can't devote all my time to you."

"Every time I come to see you now, you get up from your chair as if to show me that it is time to leave." She breathed a deep breath. "Very well - I now ask you to cancel the contract as my manager. I will find work on my own."

"Margaretha..."

Ignoring him, her head held high, she walked out of his office. Looking after her he raised his hands as if to say "I give up" then shook his head.

December 14, 1912

MUSIC CRITIC, Paul Oliver stood at the podium on the stage in the auditorium of the Université des Annales in Paris, looking out over large audience.

"I am here tonight," Oliver said to the crowd, "to address the

members of the Université on the subject of Japanese, Indian, and Javanese temple festivals."

"Mata Hari, the famous dancer, will appear, to, in a sense, underline my words in movement. She will perform the "The Princess and the Magic Flower" along with a new dance which she calls "Chundra" to be danced by moonlight. The orchestra is directed by Music Master of the Maharajah of Hyderabad, Inayat Khan."

"I am sure that all those present are fully aware to the noble birth of the lady you are soon to admire – and that her name is only a pseudonym.

"Born along the shores of the Ganges, she now divides her time between her tropical fatherland and her small villa in Neuilly – where she

117

isolates herself in pure Brahman fashion among her animals and flowers.

"The story of Magic Flower is one of the most popular and poetic of India. A young priestess walks in her garden, which is full of flowers. "I am walking in the garden of life" she sings. Suddenly she notices a beautiful flower, representing love. Should she pick the flower? The movements of the veil in her hands explain the struggle of her emotions. Finally, her hesitation comes to an end. The princess picks the flower – and drops her veils."

During Olivier's introduction, Madame Brisson, the director of the university de Annales, along with her female assistant, approached Margaretha backstage and looked over her costume.

"Remember Madame," the assistant said as they walked up to her, "how your father is averse to the display of too much "feminine charm" in public."

"Is anything wrong?" Margaretha, now dressed as Mata Hari, asked.

"I am afraid," Madame Brisson said to Margaretha, "that the dropping of your veils might reveal, how to put it delicately, a bit too much of the female anatomy – which in turn might shock some of the more reserved patrons present."

"But the introductory music has started." Margaretha said.

Madame Brisson frantically rummaged through the dressing rooms – finally coming across a long piece of red flannel. As the astonished dancer looked on, the red cloth was hurriedly wrapped around her like a diaper.

Her musical cue sounded. With no choice in the matter, Margaretha, red diaper and all, emerged onto the stage before an astonished audience and performed her dance.

Chapter 12

"People do not understand..."

❖ ❖ ❖

February 20, 1913

WITH THE FIASCO of the Université des Annales still weighing on her mind and the relentless bill collectors on her doorstep, Margaretha needed money, she once again sought the help of her former agent.

"Can't we just let bygones be bygones?" She pleaded.

"Alright. I'll do what I can." He told her. "But I'm letting you know right now - I can no longer obtain the top bookings and high salary you were accustomed to."

"That's all right." She said, relieved. "I am available to dance at any private parties – whatever the price. I leave the question of money entirely up to you."

"Whatever the price?"

"If you feel say, one thousand francs, is too much, then ask for six hundred. Or even less. I am desperate for work."

"Okay – there I may have a job for you – but it is in is in a field you haven't tried before."

"What is that?"

"Musical comedy."

Margaretha looked at him – tried, but could not find a response.

"*Le Minaret* is in the middle of a successful run at the Théâtre de la Renaissance. For the fiftieth performance, the producer of the play, Madame Cora Laparcérie, wants to treat the public at the Nuptial Festival to something special. She's specifically asked for Mata Hari to, in her words, 'brighten the third act.'"

Margaretha smiled.

April 18, 1913

HER LAST VAIL fluttered to the floor – and Mata Hari stood naked to the world. The standing applause that followed brought down the house. Margaretha swelled with pride – then bowed to her cheering audience. After soaking in the applause for several minutes, she lifted he vails and finally walked off the stage.

In the wings, as Margaretha slipped on the dressing gown offered her by a stage hand, Madame Laparcérie approached her. The applause was just now starting to die down.

"What are you doing, say, for the next month?" Madame Laparcérie asked Margaretha.

"Why? Do you have something in mind?"

"How would you like to repeat this performance three times a week until my engagement at the Théâtre de la Renaissance is up on May 18th?"

"One thousand francs per appearance?"

Madame Laparcérie laughed. "If but I could. I'm sorry my dear, but I can only offer you the same pay as the other performers. You understand."

Margaretha nodded – then hesitated. The fact that her stable of horses and villa were a continual drain on her – and that no other offers were forth coming – quickly made up her mind.

"Agreed." Margaretha told her – and they shook hands.

The addition of Mata Hari to the third act of *Le Minaret* proved to be a smart move on Madame Laparcérie's part – the show almost immediately began to be sold out every night.

On May 18 the play's engagement at the Théâtre de la Renaissance was over. But instead of ending the play's run, the sold-out crowds convinced Madame Laparcérie to simply move it to another theater, the Comédie des Champs Élysées, keeping Mata Hari in the third act.

June 26, 1913

IT WAS DURING this night in an interview with Eugéne d'Aubigny in her dressing room that Margaretha, as Mata Hari demonstrated her annoyance at the medium of comedy. What had started as a serious performance of Javanese dance had become part of a comedic play. And while no one laughed, she sensed they didn't appreciate it either. It was the closing night of *Le Minaret* and Margaretha saw no harm in expressing her true thoughts to the journalist.

"People do not understand." Mata Hari told d'Aubigny. "The public sees only the gestures, but does not understand the meaning. To execute our dances, one needs our education which was shaped through tree thousand years. Our dances require moonlight and palm trees – they are lost on a stage."

"In our country we too have dancing girls who serve the pleasures of men. But the real ones, the sacred ones, are respected and never touched. If a Hindu feels any sensual emotion when contemplating a dancing girl, he reserves it for the woman who is accompanying him."

After the interview, at first Monsieur d'Aubigny wondered if it was even worth his while to stay for the performance. But he did – and she didn't disappoint him. He was "perfectly charmed" as he put it, and followed "the development of the symbolic and ideal poem" danced "with expressive gestures."

June 28, 1913

Mata Hari was once again hot property.

Ad for "La Revue en Chemise" at the Folies-Bergere - June 28, 1913

Then Gabriel Astruc received a request asking if Mata Hari would make a one-time appearance in the show *La Revue en Chemise*. Among the audience would be the Brazilian Ambassador, princes, counts, and the foremost actors in Paris.

This would be a complete change of venue for the dancer. Gone were the temples of India and the dances of Java. Dressed in a Habanera, her body would be tightly enclosed in a corset with a wide Spanish skirt hiding her legs as she danced against a backdrop copied from a painting by Goya.

Margaretha did not disappoint her audience. "Her arms, supple as lianas, have been preserved for us, as well as her face with the large eyes and the fine feline lips" read the review - and the sold-out house gave Mata Hari a standing ovation. Not one to dismiss such a crowd, she gave them an encore performance.

Although booked only for a single night, the producer of *La Revue en Chemise* knew a good thing when she saw it. In the wings under the thunderous applause, she signed Margaretha for the entire summer season.

With a steady paycheck for the next two months added to her total earnings for *Le Minaret*, by September 1, 1913, when the show closed Margaretha made less than half of what she once commanded for a single performance. And nearly every penny was spent maintaining her stable of horses and the up-keep on her villa. Money had become a treasured commodity.

After *La Revue en Chemise* closed, she began a two-week stint at the Trianon Palace in Palermo, Sicily. Heading a program of ten numbers, she appeared twice daily, followed by "cinematographic projections" and a trained dog act. After all, money was money.

September 16, 1913

RETURNING TO PARIS, Margaretha became the mistress of Constant Bazet, a Parisian banker. With his backing she sought to revive her original act with an infusion of three new Javanese dances - which she hoped to premier to the public sometime in January or February of 1914.

Learning of her plans, she was interviewed by a reporter for *Vouge* (the same fashion magazine still published today.) When asked about her life, the innocent reporter eagerly jotted down every word as if it were a statement of fact – not realizing it was just further backstory for her Mata Hari character.

"My childhood was spent at the home of my grandfather, the Regent of the island of Madura." Margaretha told her. "Through his influence, entrance to the most sacred temples was made possible, and the secret rites were thus observed. Like a child of the people, I passed from one temple to another, until the different gods and their wondrous fêtes were as familiar to me as to a native. Little by little, never thinking of a future career, but merely from the love of beauty and appeal made to an artistic nature, I schooled myself in their ways and

123

gained an understanding of the hidden meaning and the deep-seated influence of the Buddhist religions."

"In Spain I was regarded as a goddess. When I appeared in the streets every man, with the instinct of a cavalier, laid down his coat for me to walk upon. And thus, while I was in Madrid, my feet were never on the ground."

December 1913

ONE SNOWY DAY, Lieutenant Alfred Kiepert, whom she hadn't seen since their visit to Egypt together nearly seven years earlier, appeared on her doorstep. He was gladly welcomed into her parlor.

"I understand you are to be opening a new act next month." He said over coffee.

"To be honest," Margaretha replied, "over the last several months my affair with Constant Bazet has cooled – and he now says he will not finance a show. Now my only sponsor is Monsieur Emile Ètienne Guimet."

Kiepert, still maintaining his old feelings for her, saw the possibility of resuming their relationship and made his play.

"Forget the Javanese dances. Return to Berlin with me and I will help you develop a new dance - one featuring an *Egyptian* ballet."

"Egyptian... I like it." She said, reaching for the phone. Lifting the receiver, she dialed a number and waited.

"Hello?"

"Monsieur Guimet – it is Margaretha. How would you feel about the idea dropping the Javanese dances in favor of an original Egyptian ballet?"

"*Chére Madame*," He enthusiastically responded, "to stage an Egyptian ballet is an excellent idea! On the condition, of course, that it is really Egyptian. Here in Paris, you will find at the museum all the information you want."

"How about Berlin? There is a possibility I will be staying there for a while."

"In Berlin, kindly see Professor Erman at the Museum of Egyptology. His is the top-flight German museum on ancient Egyptian culture."

"Thank you, Monsieur." She hung up, then looked at Kiepert. "Berlin. I don't know... I hear a lot about the building political tensions between our countries..."

He waved her concerns off. "If it is not one thing – it is another. Come - return with me to Berlin. I will set you up in residence at the Cumberland Hotel."

Margaretha realized that if she was going to wow them with her act in Germany, then she was going to need everything in her arsenal. All her costumes and best apparel, including an array of expensive furs, filling the contents of half a dozen steamer trunks, would make the journey with her.

Vacating her "extremely charming house" at 11 Rue Windsor in the suburb of Neuilly-sur-Seine, Margaretha put her personal effects and household goods (mostly table silver and linens) in storage with the firm of Maple, at 29 Rue de la Jonquiére.

"So," Margaretha told Sister Leonide, "I went with Kiepert to Berlin and resumed my relationship with my old lover."

"And the Egyptian ballet..."

Margaretha let out a sigh of disappointment. "I looked up Professor Erman and did my research – but my idea of an original ballet - of any type - faded over the months. Now the notion resides only within the pages of my scrapbooks."

April 2, 1914

THAT EVENING, A Berlin newspaperman reported: "This day I witnessed the famous Mata Hari and one Mr. K (Kiepert) talking very animatedly and confidentially in a booth in one of the most fashionable restaurants in town. It makes me wonder if the reason she is back in Berlin is because she lost the several hundred thousand which she had once received from Mr. K as a farewell present – or whether it was love that brought her back to him."

May 23, 1914

"While my plans for an Egyptian ballet were rabidly fading," Margaretha said, "things began to look up when I signed a contract with Director Schulz to star in the play *Der Millionendieb* at the Metropole Theater in Berlin. I was to be paid forty-eight thousand marks for a six-month engagement starting on September 1st." She sighed. "Still, I had the summer to get through."

July 31, 1914

"I was dining one evening in a private restaurant room with one of my lovers, the *chef* of police Griebel, when we heard the noise of a disturbance. Griebel, who had not been informed about the meeting, took me along to the place where it was held. An enormous crowd was staging a totally mad demonstration in front of the emperor's palace, yelling *"Deutschland über Alles!"* (Germany over all!) and "All foreigners are animals!"

Griebel anxiously turned to Margaretha. "I think you should get out of Germany on the next train – while you still can."

"But Griebel - I start at the Metropol in a month. Don't you understand? I cannot go back on my word! Schulz will sue me for breach of contract!"

"To hell with the contract! If war comes the theater will close anyway! Can't you see the political situation here is turning ugly?! It's about to erupt like a volcano!"

Apprehensive but indecisive, Margaretha, the forty-eight thousand marks proving too much of a temptation, shakes her head no.

August 3, 1914,

AT DAWN, WHILE Germany was officially declaring war on France, almost the entire German army arose from the fields and marched forward in a huge wheeling movement, first through Belgium, then by the end of September, across the plains of Flanders – and directly toward Paris.

126

Not heeding the warnings of her lovers, Margaretha suddenly found herself stuck in Berlin. She also received word that day that Director Schulz had closed the Metropol and he and his family had fled the city during the night.

Once again Margaretha's plans had been thrown into disarray. Now she desperately sought to leave war-delirious Berlin and return to her beloved Paris.

August 6, 1914 – 7:00 a.m.

"I'm sorry," the ticket agent at the Berlin train station told her, "But all passenger train travel to France and Holland has been stopped."

Margaretha sighed, anxiously looking around. "In fact," He continued, "the only passenger service still open is to Zurich, Switzerland – but that's about five hundred miles from here."

"It sounds perfect to me. I'll take a one-way ticket. And what would be the most inexpensive way to ship my belongings? I have several steamer trunks."

"Ship all but your personal necessities as freight – and be sure to keep your claim ticket."

Margaretha nodded, paying the man as her trunks were loaded on-to two-wheel carts and taken to the baggage car.

Carrying with her only a carpet bag, a few minutes later she climbed aboard a passenger car crowded with other people also fleeing the city, easing herself into the only vacant seat.

The locomotive's steam whistle sounded and with a jerk the train started to move forward, steadily building up speed. It wasn't until Berlin was several miles behind them and the train was heading southward at a good clip that Margaretha allowed herself a sigh of relief and re-laxed.

All through the night and next day, the train chugged ever south-ward toward the neutral Swiss border. By 6:00 o'clock that evening, the train began to slow as it entered Schaffhausen, the last German town on the line before reaching Switzerland.

"What's going on?" Margaretha asked another passenger. "Why are we stopping?"

Her question was answered with three members of the German Secret State Police, or Gestapo (who were to take on even more terrifying attributes in WW II) climbed on board and started down the aisles.

"Papers!" The trenchcoated leader of the team announced to the passengers. "I need to see your official identification papers before you can be allowed to leave the country!"

One by one the people pulled their travel documents from their clothing and one by one the special papers were carefully checked over.

Finally, the intense man approached Margaretha.

"Papers." He said, holding out his hand.

She looked at him then handed him her passport and visa.

"This is no longer enough. I want your special identification papers."

"I don't have any. But just let me travel though and I will leave Germany forever and you'll never have to deal with me again."

"You're coming with me." He raised his hand and gestured to his cohorts. Margaretha was roughly pulled from her seat and dragged from the train.

On the train depot's platform, the man signaled to the locomotive and it began to chug its way out of the station.

"But - my luggage!" Margaretha shouted as she was led into the back of an open car and driven away.

What she didn't know until later was that her trunks had not been sent on as freight – they had been confiscated by the Gestapo at Schaffhausen, and thoroughly searched. Not finding anything incriminating, she was detained overnight then put aboard the same train the following day as it made its return trip to Berlin.

On the evening of the tenth, she found herself back in Berlin, this time alone and penniless. Her first though after getting off the train, was to contact the Police Chief, Herr Griebel by phone.

128

"Please help me." She pleaded. "I was refused entry to Switzerland – even though my luggage continued across the border."

"New border restrictions have been put into effect." The police chief told her curtly. "From this time forward official identification papers are needed to enter the country."

"I know that now. But what can I do?" she asked. "I'm back in Berlin - alone with only the clothes on my back and no money!"

"That is not my concern. But be warned – you are now on our watch list."

"Watch list? What watch list? What are you talking about?"

"Do not bother trying to contact me again. I can no longer help you." With that he hung up.

Hanging up, Margaretha nervously paced up and down the lobby of the Cumberland Hotel. Once again, her world was crashing in around her. Her home in Paris was out of reach as the Germans continued their steady march toward the city. She had no money and no prospects of performing again any time soon.

Then a middle-aged gentleman, forever identified as Mr. K[7], noticed the desperate and anxious actions of the exotic good-looking woman.

"May I be of any assistance?" He asked, approaching her.

At first, she just looked at the man, unsure anymore of whom to trust – then the desperate soul broke down.

"I am a dancer." She finally told him. "I was supposed to appear at the Metropole Theater when war was declared." She looked around. "I'm Dutch, but because I have lived in Paris for many years, the German police suspect me of being unfriendly to their country. They confiscated all my money and all my valuable furs!"

"What can I do?"

"I've had my fill of Berlin!" She sobbed. "I just want to go home to Holland - but now they claim I haven't the right identity papers."

---

[7] Not to be mistaken for Lieutenant Alfred Kiepert. This Mr. K was a different person.

"Calm down, my dear." He told her, trying to comfort her. "I too, am Dutch. I know the Dutch consulate in Frankfurt – he can get you the papers you need to cross the border. I will call him and explain matters."

"Thank you." She sighed. "But I don't have money for train fare to Frankfurt."

"Then I will leave you a ticket for tonight's train at the hotel desk."

"Will you be coming with me?" She asked.

"No, I'm afraid not, my dear." He said with a chuckle. "My wife would not approve of me traveling alone with such a beautiful woman."

He guided her to one of the lobby desks that contained a pen and sheets of paper with the Cumberland Hotel logo on each sheet.

"This is my name and address in Amsterdam." He told her. "When you've saved enough to pay me back," He said, folding the paper and holding it out, "send it here."

Taking the folded piece of paper, she was unsure of what to say – when he tilted his hat, smiled and walked away.

She caught the train to Frankfurt that evening. As the train rumbled the three hundred miles south-west through the night to its destination, the rhythmic jostling of her passenger car caused the exhausted Margaretha to quickly fall asleep in her seat.

Arriving the next morning fully refreshed, the 38-year-old went to the Dutch Embassy and, as Mr. K. promised, found a travel document good for one year and a train ticket to Amsterdam waiting for her. With no reason to linger there, after being in the city for only a couple of hours she boarded the next train to Amsterdam.

The countryside rushed past her passenger car window all day long before the train arrived on the Atlantic coast of Holland late that afternoon, about two hundred and twenty-five miles from Frankfurt.

Stepping out of the main train terminal onto the busy streets of Amsterdam, Margaretha paused. She suddenly realized she was not only penniless – she didn't have any place to go. Adam Zelle, her father, had died five years earlier, and his second wife loathed her. Although her brothers lived in the city, she hadn't kept in contact or corresponded with either of them in years.

Pulling the folded paper from beneath her blouse, Margaretha glanced at the address. Knowing no one else in town, she went to see Mr. K and his wife.

During this initial visit, Mrs. K soon found herself warming up to the unhappy, lonely woman.

"What am I going to do? My financial circumstances are worse than ever." Margaretha told her over a cup of tea that afternoon.

"Yes, I imagine it will be difficult for you to get readjusted to life here in Holland." Mrs. K. responded. Food is becoming scarce which has caused the government to impose a rigid system of rationing."

"What? Rationing? In a country rich with dairy products?!"

"Before the war - yes. But now there is neither butter nor cheese to be found."

"Why not?"

"Everything in storage has been purchased either by the allies or Germany and much of the milk giving cattle has been butchered for meat. Now we have to make do with bad margarine and some kind of worse cheese spread. White bread is becoming a luxury. The potatoes are soggy and eggs are of a preserved putrefied kind."

"I didn't realize..."

"That's not the worst of it. Being neutral, like Switzerland, tens of thousands of Belgian refugees are now streaming across our border every day. Our schools have been closed to house them. They even

131

have field kitchens set up in front of the school buildings where long lines form every day."

"It sounds as though I may be joining them..."

"Not if I can help it. I'll convince my husband to put you up at the Victoria Hotel here in Amsterdam."

"I just hope you will allow me to spend many an evening with you and your husband here at your home."

"Miss Zelle, I am well aware of your reputation with men. Would you give me an honest answer to a question?"

"If I can."

"My husband is a distinguished, good-looking man. To thank him for his generosity, were you tempted to seduce him?"

"To be completely honest - no."

"And why not?"

"Because I had only one chemise left, as everything else had been taken away from me – and really, I didn't feel clean enough."

Mrs. K. smiled. "Thank you for being so candid."

September 1914

IT HAD BEEN eight long years since Margaretha had seen her daughter, Non, for those few minutes at the Arnhem railway station. Now the little girl was a 16-year-old young lady who knew relatively little about her mother. What she had heard was from John and wasn't good.

While in Amsterdam, Margaretha strolled past John's house on several occasions, making note of the "lovely curtains in front of the windows" yet she seemingly made no efforts to get in touch with Non – until one morning...

Margaretha knocked on the front door. The housemaid answered.

"Yes ma'am?"

"I'd like to talk to Nonnie Zelle, please."

The maid looked Margaretha up and down.

"And whom shall I say is calling?"

"Her mother."

"One moment."

The door shut and Margaretha stood nervously waiting on the doorstep for a moment.

The door abruptly open again – and John, now in his sixties and looking old, stood looking at her. Margaretha caught a brief glimpse of Non in the room behind him.

"It is you... What do you want?" He asked curtly.

"I'd like to explain to my daughter any rumors she may have heard about me. I believe she's old enough now to hear my side of the story."

"If you want to see her, you talk to me first."

"I'm talking to you, aren't I? Now be good enough to let me see my daughter!"

John pondered her request for a moment.

"All right. I don't see any reason why not. I no longer feel any bitterness towards you." Margaretha snorted. "Just pay for our round-trip tickets and you can meet her at the train station in Rotterdam."

"Rotterdam?! She's right behind you! Why can't I see her now?"

"Because I read the newspapers! I know all about you! All you want to do is parade around Amsterdam or The Hauge and show her off! Well, I won't have it! Nobody knows you in Rotterdam..."

"But I can't afford to pay for three round trip tickets..."

"I should have known..." He said, shaking his head. "You haven't changed one bit. You expect *me* to pay for them, don't you?!"

"No! I only want..."

She was cut off when the door was slammed in her face. Stepping back onto the street, tears welling in her eyes, Margaretha walked away, to never so much as glimpse her daughter again.

October 15, 1914

IT WAS DURING one of their almost daily cups of tea together that Margaretha introduced Mrs. K. to one Mr. Soet and revealed her long term plans.

"This is Mr. Soet." Margaretha told Mrs. K. "I hope you don't mind, but I've invited him here today to take care of some business, of which I'd like you to be witness."

"Please sit down, Mr. Soet." Mrs. K. told him.

"Mr. Soet is a contractor who works out of The Hague. When I heard he was going to be here in Amsterdam I asked him to meet me here – I hope you don't mind."

"Not at all, dear."

"As I've already explained to Mr. Soet, I've decided to leave Amsterdam and move to The Hague. I've rented a small house at 16 Nieuwe Uitleg, along a beautiful, quiet canal. But before I can move in, a lot of work has to be done on the old building."

"Such as?" Mrs. K. asked.

"Renovating and redecorating, mostly." Mr. Soet explained. "The most expense arises in installing a bathroom where none existed before."

"I see." She glanced at Margaretha. "Do you mind me asking why you are leaving?"

"As you know Mrs. K., dancing is my chosen profession. Over the past couple of months I've been approached by various theatrical producers. Yesterday, I signed a contract with one Mr. Roosen. I am to dance at the Royal Theater in The Hauge on December 14."

"Ah." Mrs. K. smiled and nodded. "And there is little sense in you living here if you're performing there."

"Now, Mr. Soet. Before I accept your proposal, I want it to be understood that your honest and approved bill will be paid in full within two years from the day I move into the house."

"I understand."

"But I must be free to pay the amounts I have at my disposal during that time, whether they be large or small."

"Sounds reasonable."

Margaretha then signed the contract with Mrs. K. looking on. Mr. Soet smiled, folded up the document and got to his feet.

"If you'll pardon me, ladies." He said, tipping his hat.

"And while I'm waiting for the house to be finished," Margaretha explained to Mrs. K., "I'll change hotels. From the Victoria Hotel here in Amsterdam to the Hotel Paulez in The Hague."

"My God be with you, my child."

FOR THE NEXT nine months, now living in The Hague at the Hotel Paulez, Margaretha danced at whatever venues she could, and engaged in several love affairs. She had become, by this time, uncompromisingly promiscuous "but in a ladylike sort of way." A successful courtesan known more for her sensuality and eroticism than for her classical beauty, she was genuinely fond of some of the men– the others kept her in money.

One lover that stood out was 52-year-old Baron Edouard Willem van der Capellen, who was a distinguished member of the Dutch aristocracy and had just become a full Colonel and commander of the Corps of Hussars.

"Van de Capellan was a dear, but he only visited me on the weekends. No glamor anywhere in times of war."

As the months dragged on, inactivity was starting to get on Margaretha's nerves - as was being put off from moving into her new home by one delay after another. She disliked the quiet small-town atmosphere of The Hague – complaining to Edouard that "there are not enough theaters in Holland."

By August of 1915 her outstanding bills, first to the Hotel Victoria, and now to the Hotel Paulez, had steadily accumulated to the princely sum of just over 4,000 guilders.

August 8, 1915

ERNST HIJMANS was a lawyer whose offices sat only a few doors down from Margaretha's house on the Nieuwe Uitleg. He was busy going over paperwork that morning when a rapid knocking came from his front door. Opening it, he found a flustered 39-year-old dancer standing on his doorstep.

"Miss Zelle." He said cordially. "What can I do for you?"

"Mr. Soet appeared at my door at the Hotel this morning," she told him, marching into his office, "and asked me to sign a statement in which I was to confirm that I owed him 400 guilders."

"Okay..."

"But just last night I learned he'd been making the rounds visiting my friends trying to get them to countersign for me! Why would he do such a thing?!"

"Obtaining their signature would have enabled him to use the paper as a promissory note at a bank."

"You mean..."

"Yes. He could have cashed it in immediately and received actual money."

"I knew it was something like that! That makes me so angry! He trusted me when he started, and now, a year later, he should not be trying to get my signature as a guarantee!"

She paused her ranting and glanced at Hijmans.

"I just found out he has tried to get a loan on this paper even before he had it in his hands! And none of my friends want their names used for such a purpose. Now, of course, no one will sign because they have been warned."

"I must be free to pay the amounts I have at my disposal, whether large or small. It was *these conditions* that I accepted his proposal in Amsterdam, in the presence of Mrs. K, and he had better keep his word, or he can remove everything – but – I reserve the right to sue for damages – *and* for the dirty work with the bill – *and* for the long sojourn in hotels."

She reached into the boddice of her dress and pulled out a folded paper. "Here," she said, handing it to Hijmans.

"What is it?"

"A bill from the carpenter - intended for Mr. Soet, but sent to me. I'm tired of these people coming to the Hotel, bothering me with this sort of thing. After all, I don't know them."

"It sounds to me as if he isn't paying his crew."

"If Mr. Soet does not want to keep his word, I would rather he took everything he brought into the house out again. Such people are dangerous and I did not come here to have lawsuits and all kinds of trouble."

"Is the house at all livable?"

"Well, yesterday VanBurgh finally installed the bathtub. The gas company has fixed the meter and I now have gas. My friend Anna and I are scheduled to do a final check of the completed house today - but I shall only move in when I know where I stand with Soet!"

"You leave the business side of things with me and go ahead with the final check of the house. I'll make sure the contractor sticks to his side of the agreement."

"Thank you."

Margaretha exited the house/office and stepped into the street of the Nieuwe Uitleg and walked up to Anna Lintjen, who stood waiting for her several houses down.

Margaretha joined Anna, pausing and gathering her thoughts together.

"Is he here?" She asked Anna.

"Inside. He just brought in a mattress." Anna made a sour face. "It had a funny smell to it even out here."

"We'll see about that."

Entering the house, Margaretha and Anna saw the workmen finishing the final touches on the trim and placing furniture. Heading to the upstairs bedroom where the mattress had been installed, they brushed past two men about to carry a wardrobe up the stairs.

Entering the bedroom, they found Mr. Soet adjusting the horsehair mattress into the bed frame. It took but one sniff to make Margaretha wince.

"*That* is not the kind of bed I am accustomed to." She said to Mr. Soet, covering her nose.

"Why not?!" Mr. Soet declared, acting offended. "It is of excellent quality! Filled with the best horsehair I have been able to lay my hands on!"

Margaretha flew into a rage. She reached into her purse, and pulling out a nail file, cut the mattress open with a single slash. Grabbing a

137

handful of smelly old horsehair, she yanked it out and held it under the nose of the astonished Mr. Soet.

"So *that's* what you call good quality?!"

Stomping out of the room, Margaretha encountered the two men resting at the top of the landing after carrying a wardrobe up the stairs.

"Where do you want this?" One of the men asked her.

"In there." She said, gesturing to the bedroom.

Mr. Soet looked at the wardrobe then studied the door opening. "It won't go, Madame." He told her.

"It won't go?!" Margaretha then shoved the wardrobe and watched it break into pieces as it tumbled down the stairs. "Looks like it went to me."

Margaretha moved into the house on August 11, 1915 and, as Mata Hari, became registered as a resident of The Hague at the Vital Statistics Office (and remains so to this day.)

But her financial situation did not improve immediately. Throughout September she was visited numerous times by the bookkeeper of the Hotel Paulez seeking payment of her hotel bill. Each visit ended in the same manner with Margaretha telling him he could have full confidence in her.

As late as October 8, 1915, two months after she moved out of the Hotel, she wrote a letter to the hotel's director telling him that she would "pass by one of these days, probably next week" and settle her accounts.

And Margaretha had reason to be optimistic. Throughout the summer various theatrical producers had been approaching her - but for one reason or another she rejected the offers. Sit wasn't until mid-October she finally signed a contract with one Mr. Roosen, owner the Royal Theater in The Hauge, for two performances.

December 14, 1915

FOLLOWING THE OPERA, Margaretha, as Mata Hari, made her debut at the Royal Theater in The Hauge. The 38-year-old performed a variation of her Dance of the Severn Veils "which fluttered transparently around her" – this time under strict orders not to drop the last two, a white and dark-red veil.

As the theater owner, Mr. Roosen, had hoped, the people came to the theater in droves. All seats were sold out, making her appearance "the most packed house we have had this season." Roosen was happy. The cashier was happy. It could not have been better.

A repeat performance took place at the Municipal Theater in Arnhem four days later, on December 18. It too, was a sell-out.

Not only was Margaretha able to pay off much of her debt, her wages for the two shows finally allowed her to make a quick trip to Paris in late December to recover the ten wooden packing crates containing her personal effects and household goods (mostly table silver, linens, and some furniture) which had been left in storage now for over two years.

At least, that's the reason she gave everyone for her return to Paris. In truth, she was bored - she needed the stimulation of the big city.

"How I longed for Paris! For the excitement – the luxury!"

December 20, 1915

ON THAT CHILLY afternoon in December, Margaretha's train boarded the S.S. *Hollandia,* the boat-train (ferry) for Dieppe, a voyage that required a changeover in England.

It's boilers hissing, with clouds of steam filling the platform, the train pulled into the depot at Folkestone. With the sound of slamming carriage doors, Margaretha pulled her coat tight around her against the chill as she and the other passengers disembarked amid the shouts of porters and the clatter of carts. They made their way to the immigration shed where she and the rest of the passengers were questioned by Frank Bickers, a British Police Sergeant, under the watchful eyes of Captain Dillon, an intelligence officer from MI5, and the usual customs and immigration men. One by one the people were question, cleared, and sent back to the train. Finally, it was her turn.

"Name?" Bickers asked, looking over her passport.

"Margaretha Zelle-Mcleod."

"The nature of you trip?"

"I am enroute to Paris to retrieve the effects from my house at Neuilly - which have been in storage."

Unbeknownst to Margaretha, as she was being questioned, Bickers' men were searching through her copious amount of luggage. One of the men working under Bickers now approached him and took him aside.

"Sir, we searched her luggage thoroughly..." The man informed him.

"And?" Bickers asked.

"We found nothing incriminating."

"Still," Captain Dillon said, making himself part of the conversation, "she is to be regarded as, shall we say, not above suspicion. Her subsequent movements should be watched. As far as I'm concerned she should be refused permission to return to the United Kingdom."

"But why?" the man asked.

"She's a whore. Isn't that enough? Not exactly the picture of moral rectitude, is it?"

"Sir?"

"Haven't you ever heard of the dancer Mata Hari." Bickers asked.

"So that's her. I've heard stories of her stripping it all off in front of them high-powered politicians, playboys, aristocrats, even royalty. Imagine that - all kinds of rich people just there to see a pair of bristols and a beard."

"Handsome, bold type of woman." Bickers said, looking her over. "Well and fashionably dressed. According to her passport, she speaks French, English, Italian, Dutch and some German."

"That hardly makes her above suspicion, now does it?" Captain Dillon asked. She's still a whore. And a whore will do anything for money – for whatever she thinks will get her ahead."

"Don't take no stretch of the imagination to see her spying for the Huns, does it?"

"It does not. That is exactly how whores behave." Captain Dillon shook his head and gave her a disgusted look. "Most unsatisfactory..."

PARIS LURED Margaretha like a butterfly to light. She assured Baron Edouard Willem she was only going to collect her belongings, then ship them back to The Hague. But once amid the lights and excitement in Paris she kept finding excuses to stay – especially after renewing an old love affair with Henri de Marugerie.

Then one day she met Marquis de Beaufort in the lobby of the Grand Hotel.

"The attraction was immediate, mutual, and intense." She recalled. "Good reason to linger."

She visited her agent, Gaberiel Astruc just after the New Year, in hopes of returning to the Paris stage – but, with the war commanding precedence over everything in 1916, no one in the entertainment business was interested.

Still, everywhere she went, like a modern-day movie star, she couldn't help but attract attention. Tidbits about her being sited at this event or that restaurant appeared almost weekly in the Paris press – and gained the interest of various intelligence offices. The German, British and French intelligence services in particular, wary of the smartly dressed, flagrant, self-confident 39-year-old, began shadowing her every move. As she made her way between the restaurants, parks, tea shops, boutiques, and nightclubs, it wasn't long before Margaretha noticed that she was being followed.

Soon tiring of the constant vigil, she decided not to put off her return to The Hague any longer. In January of 1916 she returned to Holland, but because the war continued to block any direct passage of her and her ten wooden crates, she was forced to take the round-about route through Spain and Portugal.

In Madrid, Spain, she took the opportunity, and a few days, to hook up with another lover, Emilio Junoy, the Spanish senator.

Once back in Holland, the first visitor at her house on the Nieuwe Uitleg was Baron Edouard Willem van der Capellen. Their weekend romance was rekindled - but Margaretha soon found The Hague as dull in 1916 as it had been the year before. Although it was a relief not to be followed wherever she went, she soon bored of the quiet small-town atmosphere, once complaining to Edouard that "there are not enough theaters in Holland."

With Paris once again calling to her like a lover, Margaretha applied for a new passport from the Dutch government in February. An entrance visa for France was easily obtained from the French Consul in Holland – but there were difficulties with the needed British visa.

On April 27, 1916, she went to the Foreign Office in The Hague to ask for assistance. She was told to return home because it might take several days. She'd be notified by telegram when her visa was granted.

Later that day the Foreign Office sent a telegram to the Netherlands Legation in London:

"Well-known Dutch artist Mata Hari, Netherlands subject whose real name is McLeod-Zelle wants to go for personal reasons to Paris where she has lived before the war. British consul Rotterdam declines to put visa to passport though the French consul has done so. Please beg British government to give orders to consul Rotterdam that visa may be granted."

Although the telegram arrived in London that afternoon, for reasons unknown, it was not delivered to the home office until six days later, on May 3, leaving the British only 24 hours to answer. And they did:

"Visa refused. Authorities have reasons why admission of lady mentioned in telegram in England is undesirable."

British suspicion of Margaretha was based on their reports from their agents in Holland, who had informed their superiors in London about a visit she had received in The Hague on her return from her first visit from one of the German consuls in Amsterdam (Mr. K.) she received in The Hague on her return from her first wartime trip to France.

The fact that there were no laws prohibiting a Dutch national in neutral Holland from talking to a German subject, the meeting raised definite suspicion in the circles of British Intelligence. For the past year they had considered her a definite suspect. Undeterred, she made the trip anyway.

Margaretha received her new passport on May 15, 1916. The steamship *Zeelandia* left Holland on May 24, 1916, and the first date stamped into her new passport was June 12, 1916, when she entered Madrid, Spain.

On June 14, she left Madrid by train for Paris – but it was stopped in Hendaye, on the French side of the border. The intelligence Service in Paris, "warned" by the British, tried to keep an eye on their suspect and had advised the authorities in Hendaye not to let her back into the country.

"I am sorry, madame." The French gendarme told her. "I cannot let you back into France."

"But why?!" Margaretha asked as the anger built within her.

"I do not know, Madame." The Frenchmen told her. "I suggest you go and ask for help from the Dutch consul in San Sebastian."

"I will do better than that! May I use your telephone?"

"Why?"

"I would like to place a call to an old friend."

"We cannot allow personal calls."

"Then I'd like your name and badge number."

"Again – why?"

"So, I can give it to my friend, Monsieur Jules Cambon when he asks. You know, the secretary-general of the French Foreign Office? You may have heard of him..."

The nervous guard ran his hand over his face then looked at her.

"That will not be necessary." He said, stamping her passport.

With that, Margaretha had no further trouble at the French border and continued on to Paris.

Chapter 13

"I never felt like this about a man before..."

❖   ❖   ❖

TWENTY-FIVE YEAR-OLD Russian Captain Vladimir de Maslov[8] of the first Russian Special Imperial Regiment was called up to be part of the fifty-thousand-man Expeditionary Force Russia sent to the Western Front. He arrived at the Maya camp in Champagne, France, on July 1, 1916.

Maslov, originally an ensign, had been promoted to warrant officer in the army infantry by Supplement to the VP February 1, 1915, and sent to serve in the 4th company of the 49th Infantry Reserve Battalion.

On February 24, 1915, he left for the front with the Russian expeditionary force, the 51st Marching Company in Lvov, a member of the 8th Infantry Regiment. On November 5, 1915, he was promoted to Second lieutenant for his actions during an attack on a fortified position near the village of Kosmerzhin on June 6, 1915.

"To Vadim Maslov," his citation read, "for the fact that, commanding a company and securing the right flank of the entire combat sector, by breaking through, under deadly rifle and machine-gun fire, through three rows of barbed wire and, after a fierce bayonet fight, bursting into

---

[8] Spelled 'Massloff' in the French

144

the trenches and personally capturing an operating machine gun. Having then repulsed several fierce attacks by the superior enemy, he launched a counterattack and captured twelve German officers, four hundred and fifty prisoners of lower rank and two machine guns, which contributed to the overall success of the business."

For his heroic actions, he received the Order of St. Vladimir, 4th class with swords and a bow on September 17, 1915, and the Order of St. George 4th class on May 23, 1916.

July 26, 1916

ON LEAVE IN Paris, Maslov was waiting for his scheduled promotion to Staff Captain on August 1, 1916, when he visited Madame Dangevill's salon. It was there, across a crowded room that the dashing Second Lieutenant's eyes met the gaze of Margaretha's. This was by all accounts, a case of love at first sight.

Margaretha couldn't help but stare at young, uniformed officer, his chest full of medals. And when his head turned and their eyes met, for the first time in her life she felt an overpowering magnetism she'd never experienced before toward any man.

Up until this time, sex had been a casual thing with no meaning beyond the coupling, or just another tool she used to get what she wanted from men. While she may have left a trail of broken-hearted men across the European continent, Margaretha herself was emotionally indifferent towards her lovers – until now.

Seeing this exotic, enticing woman studying him across the crowded room, a sudden passion ignited within Vadim – a fire he'd never experienced before. He walked directly over to her, never taking his eyes from hers.

Coming face to face, he paused in front of the plumpish forty year-old, studying the intensity in her eyes. Then, without a word, he gently took her in his arms - and they kissed. Surrendering to him like a long-lost lover now rejoined, she tightly embraced the man. To the couple, the world fell away - the other people in Madame Dangevill's salon no longer existed – only their passion surrounded them in the moment.

145

After their kiss, he pulled away slightly and looked at her, his heart pounding in his chest.

"I...I..." he stammered. "I couldn't help myself."

Margaretha just looked in his eyes. "My god..." She told him, panting, "I've...I've never felt like this about a man before! What is your name?"

"Maslov – Vladimir Maslov. And yours?"

"Margaretha Mac... Zelle. Margaretha Zelle." They kissed again.

"I don't know why," She told him, "but I feel an overpowering need to be with you, to touch you, love you..."

"I could not have said it better."

"Then let us not waste time." She told him. "I've got a room at the Grand Hotel..."

To anyone who has been in love, no description of their intense union that followed is necessary. To those that haven't been, no length of words describing their actions can convey the powerful emotions that engulfed the couple. Suffice to say that neither left the hotel room for the next seven days.

Maslov lay in the king-size bed in the darkened room with Margaretha cuddled on his chest – the sheets and blankets in total disarray - their clothing on the floor all around them.

"I love you, Marina.[9]" Vadim said, catching his breath.

"I love you, too." Margaretha said, cuddling up to him. She then lifted her head and looked at him with surprise. "I just realized - I have never said that to any man before!"

"Nor I to any woman." Vadim said, taking a deep breath, "But I must leave."

"Now? Just as I feel all the pieces of my life are fitting together?! Vadim, *you* are the love of my life."

"I feel the same, Marina, but I have no choice. Tomorrow is the 4th of August and as a captain, I *must* be at the front."

---

[9] His pet name for Margaretha

Margaretha Zelle with Captain Vladimir Maslov

Sliding out of the bed, he stood up then stepped into the bathroom and adjusted the hot water in the shower.

"I will write to you every day." She called out from the bed.

He stepped into the shower and began to wash – when the shower curtain parted and she stepped in front of him.

"What are you doing?" He asked playfully.

"Giving you a reason to return to me." She said, smiling, then kissing him passionately as the steam from the shower filled the room, fogging the mirror over the sink.

BACK IN THE trenches at the Somme in early August, Captain Maslov was ordered to lead the 4th company, assisted by thirty British tanks, some armed with machineguns, some with 6-pounder cannon, on an attack from Albert towards Bapaume between the villages of Flers and Courcellette.

With pistol in hand, the young officer raised his arm – and with rallying shout, Vadim led his men scurrying out of the trenches and onto no-mans-land, closely followed by the huge mechanical monsters that terrified the German forces.

At the same time, Margaretha, in Paris, entered Walewyk, a jewelry store. Looking into one of the display cases, she studied the selection of fine quality sterling silver cigarette cases.

But one by one, the crude lumbering tanks either broke down, became hung up in old trenches, or were knocked out by artillery. The furthest any of the armored vehicles made it was 3,500 yards into no-man's-land while murderous machinegun fire from the German lines decimated the Russian troops as they bravely hacked their way through the barbed wire.

In Paris, Margaretha casually selected a sleekly designed cigarette case, and requested Vadim's initials be engraved on it.

Then canasters of phosgene (mustard) gas were dropped among Captain Maslov and his men from Fokker triplanes flying overhead. As clouds of insidious lung and eye burning chemicals were released, the

148

attack was stopped dead in its tracks. Choking and gasping Russian troops that had survived the German machine guns now collapsed in troves, either dead or at best, completely blinded. The few survivors of the attack stumbled off the battlefield and back to their own lines as the gas cloud dispersed with the wind.

Pleased with her purchase, Margaretha exited the store onto the busy Paris streets. Enjoying the warm summer day, she strolled casually back to the hotel.

The devastated Russian troops were immediately loaded into ambulances and sent for treatment at a once luxurious spa, now turned hospital, in nearby Vittel, France. Vadim clutched his burning eyes, coughing and moaning in pain, as he was rapidly wheeled into the treatment facility by the attending nurses.

Moans of extasy emanated from Margaretha's hotel room. For, although she pined for Vladimir, in order to pay for her extravagant purchases and luxury hotel room she was forced to continue to entertain officers.

IT WASN'T UNTIL about a week later, while entertaining 27-year-old Jean Hallaure, the very tall, good-looking son of a prominent Notaire in Le Havre, that Margaretha was to learn of the gas attack...

Naked and sweaty, Hallaure rolled off Margaretha in her bed at the Grand Hotel and caught his breath.

Snuggling up to him, Margaretha laid her arm over the panting man's chest.

"And you told me your wound kept you from active duty..." She said to him playfully.

Hallaure chuckled. "Thank God I still have the lungs to breathe like this."

Margaretha raised her head and looked at him. "Whatever do you mean by that?"

149

"I'm sorry – I can't help but thinking about what happened to the 49th."

"The 49th Infantry Reserve Battalion?"

Hallaure nodded his head.

"Tell me."

He then related their experience as Margaretha listened intently.

"The survivors were rushed to Vittel." He finished. "The lives of thousands of men – for what? We've only gain three miles of ground since July first."

Margaretha sat up.

"Those poor men." She said, sliding to the edge of the bed. "And here I was planning to go to the spa there... I'll bet it's not even open to private citizens any more..."

"Yes it is." Hallaure assured her. "Only one wing of the facility has been made into a hospital. But you can't go there - Vittel is presently in the military zone."

"But I'm a citizen of a neutral country..."

"You're still a civilian. And civilians are not allowed near the fighting unless they have a special travel permit - as well as a safe-conduct pass."

The two lay in silence for a few moments.

"But I *so* want to take in the mineral waters."

"I just told you - Vittel is now in the Zone of the Armies. You're going to need a *special* travel permit and visa."

Margaretha contemplated the issue for a moment, turning to Hallaure.

She snuggled up to him. "Jean, I really need to go to the spa in Vittel... You told me you were transferred to the Intelligence Office[10] – isn't there any way you can help me?"

Hallaure thought for a moment.

---

[10] Unbeknownst to Margaretha, Jean Hallaure was actually the spy chief of the Deuxième Bureau.

"Well? Can you help me?" She asked playfully, reaching beneath the covers and fondling him.

"Okay -okay." He replied. "See a friend of mine at the Military Office for Foreigners on the Boulevard Saint Germain."

Margaretha smiled then kissed him.

"Now - let me properly thank you." She said.

T HE NEXT MORNING, Margaretha, wearing a smart summer frock and black broad-brimmed hat accented with an ostrich feather, paused her stroll down the Boulevard Saint Germain and checked the address number on the nondescript building against the one given her by Hallaure: 282 Boulevard, Foret De Saint-Germain.

Opening the unmarked door, Margaretha found herself in a dim hallway with several unmarked doors on each side, each door sporting a panel of marbled glass. Seeing only one of the rooms behind the doors was lighted within, she walked up to it, paused, then opened and entered.

She found herself face to face with the Chief of the French intelligence Service, a fat little man with a black mustache, tiny Nez Prinze spectacles, and a cigarette pasted to his lips.

Captain Georges Ladoux

She glanced at the nameplate sitting on his desk: Captain Georges Ladoux.

"Monsieur Ladoux," She said, "Jean Hallaure has sent me here to obtain a visa."

"Your name, please?"

"Margaretha Zelle-McLeod." She replied taking the seat before his desk. "But I am also known by my stage name, Mata Hari."

"Ah yes – Madame Zelle." He stood and opened a drawer in his filing cabinet. Pulling out a file, he set it on his desk, then, pushing the drawer shut, sat back down. He began thumbing through the file.

"I know all about your, how do you say, friendship, with Monsieur Hallaure. And about your relationship with Vladimir Maslov."

Surprised, she just looked at the man.

"So, you have gone through my papers?"

"France is at war, Madame Zelle, and no offense, but you are a foreigner. I would be remiss in my duties to my country if I hadn't checked you out most thoroughly."

Margaretha nodded her understanding.

"And I just want you to know," He continued, "that I do not believe for one minute the British claim."

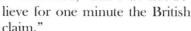

"And just what is it that the British claim?"

"That you are spying for Germany."

"What?!" She asked, laughing. "Where on earth did they get *that* notion?"

"According to my files, from your numerous travels to Berlin over the years. Right up until the beginning of the war, in fact."

Margaretha sighed. "Monsieur Ladoux, the only time I have ever visited Berlin was to perform as Mata Hari. Otherwise, I assure you, I have absolutely no interest in *anything* German."

His eyes, magnified by the lenses in his tiny glasses, studied her as he sat, thinking.

"I believe you, Madame." He said, earnestly. "Which is why I will arrange for your visa and permit to go to Vittel."

"Thank you."

"You have lived in France for almost ten years – is that not correct?"

"It is."

"But you were born in Holland. Why is it you've forsaken your home country?"

"I sought to live in Paris after my divorce. My ex is a horrible man. He refuses to even let me see my daughter."

"And what are your feelings towards France?"

"I love it here."

"Would you be willing to help the country you claim to love so much?"

"I find the idea intriguing, Monsieur Ladoux."

"And if you were to work for us, what would be the amount of your, shall I say, compensation?"

"Monsieur, I will give you an answer to that only if I decide to accept. Now, when do I get the visa?"

"I can have it for you day after tomorrow."

"Good day to you, sir."

Leaving Ladoux's office, Margaretha closed the door behind her. Hearing it shut, 39-year-old Inspector Tarlet, one of the men that had followed her in London, entered through the back door.

"Do you think it wise to give her passage to Vittel?" Tarlet asked Ladoux.

"Relax, Tarlet." Ladoux told him. "I decided I had to bring that whore down after I received warning from the British that she was a German agent. And the best way to do that is to recruit her to spy for France."

"I don't understand..."

"She's a foreigner, Tarlet. Regardless of what she says, she has no sense of loyalty to anybody but herself."

Captain Ladoux turned and looked at Tarlet.

"So, what have you got for me?"

"Monier and I have been following her all around Paris as ordered. To restaurants, dressmakers, furriers, jewelers – all over the city like a brace of bloodhounds. Sometimes she'd give us the slip, hailing taxis and carriages that made abrupt turns – even winking as she passed us going the opposite direction." Tarlet sighed. "But we were never able to get the goods on her."

"Did you steam open her mail?"

"Of course. We could find no indication of invisible ink, nor was there any writing using codes or cyphers."

"Is that all?"

"We also questioned porters, waitresses, and hairdressers, and even collected an abundant amount of information on her love affairs..."

"But no evidence of her committing espionage?"

"No sir. She was *trés elegant.*"

"What about these affairs of hers?"

"When she was staying at the Grand Hotel, they appeared to be non-stop." Monier revealed, taking out his notebook. "No sooner did the Marquis de Beaufort leave after a week with her in early July, than Bernard Antoine, a purveyor of fine liquors, appeared. And after him, a lieutenant of the Eighth Chasseurs d'Afrique followed by Russian Lieutenant Vladimir de Maslov. We saw neither head nor hair of either of them for an entire week."

"They never left the hotel?"

"They never left her *room.*"

Ladoux raised an eyebrow. "Go on."

"After Maslov left, in August she began sleeping with Jean Hallaume, another military man. He's been spending a couple of hours with her daily."

"It sounds as though she has a soft spot for military men..."

"I would say so. When she isn't with Hallaume, she's with a Belgian officer, the Marquis de Beaufort."

Ladoux shook his head. "What can I say? It is obvious you can't trust a whore in affairs of the heart."

"What are your orders, sir?"

"I want you and Monier to leave for Vittel tonight. That way when she arrives, you two will be in place to watch her every move. She knows what you two look like, so disguise yourselves – be as subtle as possible."

"Yes sir." Tarlet nodded, then turned and left.

154

OBTAINING THE SPECIAL pass and visa on July 30th, Margaretha immediately traveled by train to the spa at the foot of the Vosges Mountains near Vittel. For the next two weeks, she split her time between the health spa and clandestine meetings with her beloved Vadim.

Their first meeting was after dark in the park grounds around the spa. The only illumination being the stars overhead and the light from two gas lamps that marked the garden pathway.

Margaretha stood anxiously, waiting for Vadim when he appeared from his concealment in the tall hedges. She ran into his arms.

"How desperate I was to be with you, Vladimir!" She said, kissing and embracing the young man.

"And I with you, Marina."

"What happened to you?!" She asked, pausing and looking at the patch over his left eye.

"It was either the Germans or the Turks." Maslov explained. "After leading a charge across No Man's Land, they hit us with mustard gas! I barely made it back to our lines alive."

"Such insidious chemicals! Is it bad?"

"I am blind in my left eye - and very nearly in my right." He heaved a deep sigh. "I will never lead men on the battlefield again."

"I don't care about that, Vladimir." She said, stroking his hair. "At least we have each other."

"My injury does not bother you?"

"Of course, not - you are the same man underneath. Besides," She said playfully, "it is not your eyes I seek when I reach out for you in the middle of the night."

He smiled. "Will you marry me, Marina?" He asked.

"Yes!" She declared, throwing her arms around him and kissing him. "And I will never leave you!"

Hidden in the hedges on the far side of the garden, Tarlet and Monier trade glances - then fade into the shrubbery.

❖   ❖   ❖

When Margaretha returned from Vittel, Ladoux went about setting his trap. Tarlet and Monier returned the day after Margaretha and reported directly to Ladoux.

September 20, 1916

"Well?" Captain Ladoux asked Tarlet.

"I'm sorry, sir. But we failed to find the slightest indication that she did anything suspect or subversive. Outside of her clandestine meetings with Maslov, her conduct was - exemplary. When she returned to Paris she rented an unfurnished apartment on the Avenue Henri Martin. But other than that..." Tarlet shrugged.

"Unfurnished? Does that mean she still residing at the Grand Hotel?"

"For the time being, yes."

"Very good."

"Are you really going to recruit her as a French spy for the Belgium area?"

"That is what I'll make her believe."

ANSWERING A KNOCK on her door at the Grand Hotel that morning, Margaretha opened it to find Karl Kroemer standing there, hat in hand.

"Mrs. McLeod," He said formally, "my name is Karl Kroemer. I am the German consul to Amsterdam working for the Deuxième Bureau. May I come in?"

Curious, Margaretha stepped aside and Kroemer entered her suite.

"And what can I do for you, Mr. Kroemer?"

"Did the German authorities ever return your confiscated luggage?"

"No." She said. "And now with the war on I doubt if they ever will."

"Don't ask me how, but we know you have been asked to spy for the French. Is that not so?"

156

"I do not feel it would be in my best interests to answer either way. Besides, of what concern is it of yours?"

"I know you are in debt due to your lavish lifestyle - and I am offering to pay you twenty thousand francs..."

"For...?"

"For you providing the Deuxième Bureau with any information you gain during, how shall I say it, *pillow talk* with French officers."

Margaretha leveled her eyes on the man, studying him silently for a few moments.

Sensing her hesitation, he smiled as he pulled an envelope thick with paper currency from the inside pocket of his coat – then held it out to her.

"If you like, think of these twenty thousand francs as compensation for your lost belongings."

Keeping her gaze on him, she snatched the envelope of cash from his hand. He bowed slightly, handing her a business card.

"When you have collected any information, just call the number on this card. If I am not there, they will know how to reach me."

With the twenty thousand francs clutched tightly in hand, Margaretha bowed Kroemer out the door.

Shutting the door, she turned its two deadbolts, locking them tight. With her back against the door, she opened the envelope and fanned through the paper bills.

I T WAS LATER THAT afternoon that Captain Ladoux appeared at Margaretha's door. Abruptly brushing past her, he entered her apartment as though he owned it.

"I know the real reason you wanted to visit Vittel." He told her, matter of factly as he walked into the room. "But I have no interest in your Russian boyfriend."

"Is it really necessary to have me followed everywhere?"

"It is the way the organization works."

"I see your men everywhere I look – sometimes in the most ridiculous of disguises." She walked to the window and looked down at Tarlet standing on the street corner, watching the hotel. "That man was trailing me all morning - he must be tired by now. May I suggest you allow him to go to the nearest café to at least get a drink?"

Ladoux smiled. Walking over to the window, he looked down and gestured to Tarlet, who nodded and walked away. Ladoux then turned back to Margaretha.

"Now, have you come to a decision, Madame?"

"Yes. And I realize it is dangerous to accept such missions, but have decided if anyone is able to render services to this country, it is me."

"And how much, exactly, would you consider adequate?"

"One million francs."

Ladoux raised an eyebrow.

"One million?" He asked, opening a silver cigarette case, placing one between his lips and lighting it up. "Why?"

"I want to marry Vadime." She declared. "I have no interest in all this except marrying my lover - and I want enough money that I *never* have to deceive Vadime with other men."

"Really?" Ladoux chuckled. "I thought it was because his family will only accept you if you can show them sufficient capital."

"I did you know..."

He waved her concerns off. "It is well known in certain circles that the Maslov family is almost broke – yet they still are worried he'll marry beneath his class..."

Margaretha nodded.

"I don't know..." He said, pacing the room while smoking his cigarette. "For one million francs you will have to obtain valuable information from a knowledgeable source..."

"I understand."

"It is no secret, Madame, that before the war you performed as Mata Hari several times before the eldest son of Kaiser Wilhelm II, Crown Prince Wilhelm."

"I have already been *his* mistress." She boasted. "I can do with him what I will."

"Are you sure?"

"Of course. I love officers. I have loved them all my life. I prefer to be the mistress of a poor officer than of a rich banker. It is my greatest pleasure to sleep with them without having to think of money. And, moreover, I like to make comparisons between the different nationalities."

"I want you to return to The Hague where you will receive further instructions."

"And the payment for my services..."

"*After* you have provided the information."

"Then you will excuse me, Captain Ladoux. I have to send for a cheque to pay for my hotel room before I leave."

Chapter 14

"One of the most charming specimens of female humanity..."

❖   ❖   ❖

November 7th, 1916

MARGARETHA FINALLY received a cheque for five thousand francs, a personal gift from the German military attaché Major Arnold von Kalle, sent to her by her servant, Anna Lintyens, to the Dutch consul in Paris.

Following Ladoux's instructions, the next day, after paying her extensive hotel bill, Margaretha headed for the Gare d'Austerlitz train depot in Paris.

"I'd like a train ticket to The Hague please."

"You do understand," The clerk told her, "That the war in Belgium and Germany blocks any direct route."

"I do."

"And that there are no passenger ships of neutral nations leaving from French Channel ports."

"So how do I get there?"

"You'll have to take the train to Madrid, in Spain, and from there to the coastal town of Vigo. At Vigo you can board the *Hollandia*, which is headed to Rotterdam. Once in Rotterdam you can again to take the train to The Hague."

"But that's about three times further."

The clerk shrugged. "Blame the war."

Margaretha sighed.

"How much?" she asked, reaching into her purse for the money.

THE STEAM LOCOMOTOVE pulling the morning train from Paris left a trail of smoke in the air as it streamed south across the green countryside. The train slowed to a stop at Irun just across the Spanish border, the authorities carefully checking each and every person's visa and travel documents before the train was finally allowed to proceed. Tarlet, waiting in the lobby of the Palace Hotel in Madrid, made a note that Margaretha didn't walk into the building until 7:05 p.m. that evening.

The next morning, she walked right up to Tarlet, who stood in the lobby casually reading a newspaper. With her index finger she lowered the newspaper in order to look him in the eyes.

"I recognize you from Paris." She said matter of factly. "You're following me again, aren't you?"

Tarlet, somewhat embarrassed at having been so easily spotted, stammered for a moment before collecting himself then nodding slightly.

"Just so you know," She continued, "I will be staying in Madrid for one more day. I am asking you not to follow me this afternoon because I am supposed to meet a countryman of mine between 2:00 and 4:00 o'clock. And just so you know, tomorrow I will be taking 8:13 a.m. train from Madrid to Vigo and departing for Holland from there."

"You have my word, madame." He said respectfully. "I will not follow you."

Margaretha studied the man for a moment. "Very well, then." She said, and proceed out of the hotel lobby.

As she exited the hotel, Tarlet's associate, 36-year-old Monier, wearing threadbare clothing and a grey wig and mustache, kept an eye on her as he stepped from his concealment behind a pillar to Tarlet's side.

"Follow her." Tarlet told Monier. "And be careful. She's one sharp cookie."

Margaretha enjoyed the relaxing ride in the horse-drawn cab as it made its way down the busy afternoon streets of Madrid but found the autumn morning air cool and pulled the blanket up over her lap. Neither she nor the carriage driver paid any attention to the old man in tattered clothes on a bicycle following them several carriage lengths behind.

Monier casually pedaled the bike, careful to keep the cab in view but not appear to be following it. The taxi halted before the Café Palmario and she climbed out. Pulling up on the bicycle, Monier parked it alongside the building, then stood quietly, listening.

"Driver," Margaretha told the cab driver, "Wait for me. I'll be back shortly."

The driver nodded and she went inside.

Monier casually sat down at one of the outside tables, ordering a coffee. As he sipped at his coffee, he watched Margaretha through the picture window of the café as she made two phone calls on the pay phone inside.

"And were these calls traced?" Captain Ladoux later asked Monier over the phone.

"Yes sir." Monier replied, checking his notes. "The first phone call was to the German Bank in Madrid. The second to the German consul in Vigo."

"Is that all?"

"Tarlet checked out her story – she's scheduled to take passage aboard the Dutch transport *Hollandia* tomorrow."

"Very good. You and Tarlet keep an eye on her. I'll call Captain Paul[11] and see if he will radio the British Admiralty of our suspicions."

---

[11] Chief of the French Intelligence Service

"Yes sir."

With that, Monier hung up the pay phone and left the café.

November 9, 1916 – 10:00 a.m.

S COTLAND YARD OFFICER George Ried Grant stood on the docks of Falmouth, England framed by the grey overcast skies, watching and waiting as tugboats gently nestled the Dutch steamship *SS Hollandia* into her mooring. With him was his wife, and two assisting officers, Sergeant James Crichton and Brian Percival,.

Rubbing his gloved hands together in an attempt to warm them in the chill autumn air, Grant quietly watched the proceedings as the gangplank to offboard the passengers was set in place.

"All right, Lads," He said to his officers as the passengers began to disembark, "We know she's aboard. Keep a sharp eye out."

Officers Crichton and Percival adjusted their overcoats against the cold Atlantic air and stiffened to attention as a line of people began descending the gangplank in single file.

Crichton then noticed Margaretha, striking, smartly dressed in a large black hat and long mink-collared coat, stepping onto the gangplank. He nudged Grant.

"Blimely... Will you look at that, mate?" Crichton said, pointing. "She's one of the most charming specimens of female humanity I have ever set eyes on!"

Mrs. Grant just looked at the man in disapproval and shook her head as the woman approached step by step down the gangplank.

"Don't be fooled by her glowing black eyes and dusky complexion, Sergeant." She said. "You just may be looking at the Kaiser's best method of gathering information."

"You mean – *she's* the suspected spy we've been sent here to arrest?" Crichton asked, dumbfounded.

"Don't sound so surprised, Sergeant." Grant said, glancing at the officer. "She hasn't even smiled at you – and you're already weak in the knees."

Grant approached Margaretha as she stepped from the gangplank onto the docks.

Clara Benedix

"Step over here, ma'am." He said.

"Why?" She asked, studying the man. "Who are you?"

"Officer Geroge Grant," He said, introducing himself and showing her his badge, "New Scotland Yard. May I see your passport?"

Margaretha looked at him, then pulled her Dutch passport from a jacket pocket and handed it to him.

Accepting it gracefully, he began thumbing through it.

"Why does it say here your name is Margaretha Geertruida Zelle?"

"Because that *is* my name..."

"So, you deny being the German spy Clara Benedix?"

"Really, Inspector... Do I look like a Clara?"

164

"What is your purpose in visiting England?" He asked.

"I am traveling from Spain to Holland." She told him. "I am not responsible for which ports the ship stops at in between."

"No, you are not. It was I who ordered the *Hollandia* diverted to Falmouth."

"Why, officer Grant – I'm flattered." She said, stroking his cheek. "But if you really wanted to see me that badly all you had to do was call."

Mrs. Grant gave her a wry smile. "I warned my husband about your vivacious manner and quick repartee."

"And have I met your expectations?"

"We'll see – after I've stripped searched you."

"Clara Benedix," Grant continued, "I am arresting you on suspicion of espionage." He said, looking her in the eye and holding up her travel documents. "And for having a forged passport."

Margaretha glared at him for a moment – then presented her wrists to be handcuffed.

"Behave yourself and we'll have no need for any of that." He said, gently taking her by the arm and turning to his wife. "Be sure to search her *thoroughly*." He instructed.

She nodded, leading Margaretha away.

"Sergeant Crichton – find the ship's carpenter and tell him to meet us in her cabin."

"The carpenter, sir?"

"Yes. Each of these rooms has wood paneled walls – behind which is a perfect hiding place for documents or letters. I want every inch of her cabin searched, and every panel removed. Is that understood?"

"Yes sir."

AS THE MEN emerged from her cabin after searching it, Margaretha, led by Mrs. Grant was brought before her husband.

"Well?" he asked his wife.

Mrs. Grant shook her head. "And you?" she asked him.

"Nothing." He turned to Crichton. "Sergeant, get the car. Then book us on the first train to London." He looked Margaretha in the

165

eye. "It is there, in New Scotland Yard, Miss Benedix, you will be inter-rogated at length."[12]

"Sir," Sergeant Crichton told him, "the earliest train to London doesn't leave until seven o'clock this evening."

"Fine. We'll keep her downtown."

"James," Mrs. Grant said, "You can't take her to that filthy jail – you have no restroom facilities for women."

"So, what do you suggest?"

"Have her stay with us at our lodgings here in Falmouth."

Grant was about to argue the point when his wife gave him 'the look.' Realizing he'd already lost the fight, Grant sighed and turned to Crichton.

"Sergeant!" Grant ordered. "Make sure all her luggage is offloaded before the ship is released."

"What is going on here?!" the ship's captain asked as he hurriedly approached down the gangplank. "You cannot arrest this woman! She is a neutral passenger aboard a neutral ship!"

"She's a German spy named Clara Benedix," Grant told him as Margaretha was loaded into a waiting car, "And she's going to London to the Cannon Street police station for interrogation."

"I fully intend on bringing this matter up with the authorities in Holland, inspector!" The captain shouted as the cars started away. "You are making a terrific mistake this time! This woman is the most popular passenger aboard!"

November 17, 1916

MARGARETHA, STANDING just inside the door, removed her hat while she studied the bleak interrogation room at Scotland Yard. A single electric light with a heavy metal shade hung down in the center of the room. The only furniture was a table with a folding chair set on either side of it.

---

[12] A full transcript of the interview is in Britain's National Archives

Sighing, she stepped over to the table, laid her hat on it then sat down.

Assistant commissioner at New Scotland Yard in charge of counter-espionage, Sir Basil Thomson, followed by officers Crichton and Perci-val, entered the room a few minutes later. Sir Basil paused and looked at her.

"And who are you?" she asked.

"Assistant Commissioner Basil Thomson. You know, inspector Grant is convinced you really are Clara Bénédix."

Margaretha smiled. "And just what are you convinced of inspec-tor?"

"Whoever you are and whatever your name is, I'm convinced

Sir Basil Thomson

you're spying for the Germans." He told her as he began pacing the room. "And that you are on your way - not to Holland - but to Germany with information which you have committed to memory."

"Inspector," Margaretha asked, "May I speak to you – in private?"

Sir Basil gestured and officers Crichton and Percival left the room, closing the door behind them.

"Well?" He asked.

"I freely admit I am a spy, Inspector – but not for Germany. I work for the French secret service."

Sir Basil gave her a curious look. "I don't suppose you can prove this?"

"Contact Captain George Ladoux in Paris." She said, sitting back. "He is the person who told me to go to The Hague."

"And what were you to do there?"

She shrugged. "I was to wait until I received his instructions."

Sir Basil turned and rapped on the door. Officer Crichton opened it.

"Sergeant, get one Captain Ladoux in Paris on the phone and ask if he knows..."

167

"Margaretha Zelle-Mcleod." She interjected.

"And Sergeant..." Crichton nodded and started for the door.

"Yes sir?"

"...don't come back until you receive a reply."

"Yes sir."

Sir Basil turned and paced the gloomy integration room, thinking, as Margaretha rested her head in her hands.

"You know," He said, "the three men in uniform that interrogated you yesterday tell me they suspect your accent is German."

Margaretha glanced at him. "That should tell you something. They also think I'm Clara Benedix."

He tossed a photograph of her dancing naked onto the table.

"Is this not you? The exotic dancer known as Mata Hari?"

Margaretha picked up the photograph, looked at it for a moment and sighed. "I was."

"What do you mean by that?"

"This photograph was taken in 1906." She said, looking at the inspector. "I am 40 years-old now. Time and two children have taken a toll on my figure. The last time I appeared as Mata Hari was over a year ago."

"But your passport says you're Dutch – not Malaysian or Javanese."

"Inspector," Margaretha said, taking a deep breath and letting it out, "Mata Hari is the name I used for my stage act. I am *not* a Javanese princess – I just *pretend* to be. Don't you understand?"

Sir Basil leveled his gaze at her.

"Then what is your God given name?"

"Margaretha Geertruida Zelle."

"When were you born?"

"August 7, 1876 - in Leeuwarden, Holland."

"And your mission?"

"I am to act as a French spy in German-occupied Belgium." Margaretha revealed. "I am to secure for the Allies, the assistance of Ernest Augustus, Duke of Brunswick-Lüneburg in Germany."

"Isn't he heir to the Dukedom of Cumberland in the British peerage?"

168

Margaretha shrugged. "If you say so."

The door opened again. "Inspector," Officer Crichton said, "we have Captain Ladoux on the telephone."

Sir Basil, about to leave, turned to her. "Consider yourself in custody on suspicion of espionage and on the charge of having a forged passport."

With that he left the room. Margaretha looked around and let out a deep sigh.

SIR BASIL ENTERED his office where a pedestal phone, sitting on his desk, sat with the earpiece off the hook. Parking himself in his office chair, he picked up phone.

"I'm Sir Basil Thomson, Assistant commissioner at New Scotland Yard in charge of counter-espionage. I understand the woman I have in custody works for you." Thompson said.

"You understand nothing." Ladoux replied over the phone, "I have suspected her for some time as being an agent of Germany. I pretended to employ her in order, if possible, to obtain definitive proof that she is working for the Germans. If she has orders to go anywhere, they come from them."

"That's not what *she* says..."

"Let me speak to her."

"I can't - she's not here."

"She's not in jail? What did you do with her?"

"We had to move her to the Savoy Hotel from, under guard mind you, because we have no toilet facilities expressly for women." Sir Basil sat back in his wooden office chair. "Without any evidence, I'm afraid I'm compelled to release her."

"Then send her back to Madrid."

With that, Captain Ladoux hung up. Officer Crichton entered Sir Basil's office.

"Sir, DeMatees Van Swinderen, the Netherland Minister is here to see you."

"Send him in."

"Mr. Thomson," the man said, entering the room.

"*Sir* Thomson." Sir Basil said, correcting him.

"It has come to my attention from the *Hollandia*'s captain that a Mrs. Zelle-McLeod was arrested in Falmouth on suspicion of having committed un-neutral acts and that her passport was considered to be false – and that her real nationality is considered to be German. Is that correct?"

"It is."

"I have the documents here to prove that the woman is indeed Margaretha Zelle-McLeod and that her passport was legally obtained in The Hague."

Sir Basil looked over the papers. "Okay, Mr. Swinderen. Be assured I will release her."

"Be sure you do."

Swinderen nodded, then turned and left the office.

Officer Crichton entered.

"What are your orders, sir?"

"Four days of interrogation at Scotland Yard is usually enough to crack the toughest suspect. Don't you agree, Sergeant?"

"Yes sir."

"Yet this Clara or Margaretha or whatever the hell her name is, has revealed nothing."

"She *is* proving to be a tough nut to crack."

"Or she genuinely doesn't know anything." Leaning back in his chair, Sir Basil contemplated the situation for a moment. "Let her go, Sergeant."

"But sir, the *Hollandia* set sail for the Netherlands almost a week ago."

"*Something* is going on with that woman." Sir Basil explained. "And with this war taking precedence, I've got enough on my plate. Let the French and Spanish handle it. Tell her to go back to Madrid."

"Yes sir."

Crichton entered the interrogation room, this time leaving the door wide open.

"You are free to go." He told Margaretha, standing aside.

Unsure of the man's motives, she stood up, keeping her eyes on him. "Go?" She asked. "Go where? The *Hollandia* sailed days ago."

"Sir Basil suggests back to Madrid." Crichton replied.

Without replying, she gathered her few things from the table and walked out of the room.

Dutch Embassy – London

MARGARETHA walked up to the reception desk in the embassy.

"Hello." She said, smiling. "I'm a Dutch citizen and would like a special permit to return to The Hague."

"Yes ma'am." The young man behind the counter said. "And the purpose of your visit?"

"I plan to get married."

"Congratulations. Your name?"

"Margaretha Zelle-McLeod."

"One moment." The young man then ran his finger down a list of type-written names on a paper in front of him – but because of the counter's construction, unseen by Margaretha. Spotting Margaretha's name he paused. "I'm sorry, ma'am. No special passes are available at this time."

"But..."

"Sorry. There is nothing I can do. Next!"

Frustrated, Margaretha then made her way to the Spanish consulate in London and applied for permission to go back to Madrid. The Spanish, not seeing her as a threat, granted her request. She was issued a new visa by them on November 29.

Madrid - December 15, 1916 - Morning

ONCE AGAIN TARLET stood in the pay phone booth at the Café Palmario talking to Captain Ladoux.

"She returned to Madrid on December 8 and again took a

171

room at the Palace Hotel." Tarlet told him over the phone. "From the moment she stepped ashore I've had her constantly followed by agents of the Sûreté."

"And you called just to tell me this?"

"No sir. She sought me out at the hotel this morning. She told me you had not yet paid her anything and felt that you had abused her confidence."

"I abused *her* confidence?! She promised me she'd get an interview with the Crown Prince or General von Bissing and has done neither!"

"She told me because of the fighting, she could not get an appointment with either one. She said she wrote to you telling you of her setbacks – then waited over a week for your reply, but never received one."

Captain Ladoux glanced at the envelope addressed to him lying on his desk. "I have received nothing from her." He said, sliding the envelope off the desk into a drawer and slamming it shut.

"She told me," Tarlet continued, "because she hasn't received a word from Paris and because she has only a few hundred pesetas left - while her hotel bill keeps going up and up – that she is forced to take some drastic steps."

"What did she mean by that?"

Margaretha paused on the steps of the German embassy in Madrid and contemplated her options. Feeling she had no choices left, she continued up the stairs and entered the building.

Walking up to the counter, she set her purse on it.

"I'd like an interview with the German military attaché to Madrid, please."

The clerk looked the beautiful woman over.

"Well?" She asked.

"And what is this pertaining to?"

"I am a Dutch citizen, a member of a neural country. I want to try and see whether I can manage to safeguard a trip to The Hauge through Germany without being arrested."

"I'm afraid I can't help you..."

172

"Then tell the attaché I bring him information from H-21."

The clerk's eyes widened and he lifted his phone. "One moment. I will see if Major von Kalle is in."

"And that is the information you feel is so vital?" Major von Kalle asked Margaretha now sitting in his plush office.

Margaretha sat back in the overstuffed chair, draping her arms over her crossed legs – and nodded.

"It seems I recall reading something similar in the newspapers several weeks ago..." He shrugged. "But I will pass it on."

"I was promised I would be paid..."

"How much were you expecting?"

"Ten thousand francs?"

Major Arnold Kalle

Von Kalle chuckled. "Let me cable my superiors."

Von Kalle then left the room. Margaretha took the time to study the elegant furnishings of his office, comparing them to the spartan conditions of Captain Ladoux's office.

"I'm sorry." Von Kalle told her, re-entering the room a few minutes later. "But Berlin has refused to pay you."

She sighed, looking downhearted.

He pulled out a silver cigarette case and glanced at her. "Cigarette?"

Sensing he was enamored by her, she turned on the charm. Taking a cigarette, she put it to her lips as he lit it. In her own words: "making myself very attractive. I played with my feet. I did that which a woman may do when she wishes to make a conquest of a man."

She smiled. She knew von Kalle was hers. And with that the German military attaché, in Margaretha's own words "committed some most intimate acts with me in his office."

December 15, 1916 - Afternoon

173

MAJOR VON KALLE rolled off Margaretha and laid his head on the bed pillow – then took a deep breath. As he regained his senses, he noticed the mid-day sunshine now filled the Palace Hotel room. Reaching for his pocket watch on the nightstand, he glanced at it – then sighed.

"I am sorry, Margaretha, but I must go."

"Just once more." She said, playfully, snuggling her naked body up to his and resting her head on his chest.

"Believe me, I wish I could." He said, laying his head back on his pillow and letting out a sigh. "But I'm just the Army's attaché, not a commanding officer."

She then began playfully kissing his chest. Knowing full well he'd give in if he didn't act now, he did the only thing he could.

"I'm sorry." Von Kalle said sitting up, twisting and sitting on the edge of the bed. "I'm leaving you with three thousand five hundred pesetas. But I *have* to get back."

Margaretha sighed. "But what's so important you have to leave right now?"

Kalle stood and began to pull on his clothes. "Because we've got a submarine sitting off the coast of Morocco awaiting instructions."

"I don't care about some dumb old submarine." Said she in a mocking pout.

"You don't understand, Margaretha," Von Kalle explained, slipping on his shirt. "It's loaded with German and Turk officers – not to mention munitions! We have to figure out a way of getting them ashore."

"Why do they want to come ashore?"

"To start an uprising, of course."

"Am *I* not enough to start you up-rising?"

Von Kalle looked at her and smiled. "If that's all it took, my dear, I'd only have to think of you and my mission would be accomplished."

Margaretha just smiled.

"Prove it." She said playfully.

He looked at her – sighed – and took her in his arms - his shirt sliding from his back and falling onto the floor as they passionately embraced.

174

Tired and nearly spent, Von Kalle finally left the hotel room late that afternoon. Margaretha bounded off the bed, anxious to relay the information about the submarines to Captain Ladoux. Sitting at her dressing table, she began writing down the details of her conversation with Von Kalle.

That night she triumphantly reported it to Paris.

"Now *that* must be worth the one million francs you promised me." Margaretha told Ladoux over the phone.

"We'll see."

"What do you want me to do now?"

"Sit tight and wait for my further instructions."

"But I am running out of money..."

There was a click on the other end of the phone line as he hung up. Letting out a frustrated sigh, she replaced the receiver then exited the phone booth.

As she walked out of the café, Margaretha was paused with a gesture from a man sitting at one of the tables.

"I am Colonel Joseph-Cyrille Denvignes." He told her. "I would like to talk to you, Madame Zelle."

Margaretha studied him for a moment. "I am quite indisposed at the moment." She told him. "Shall we say tomorrow, around 2:30 p.m. at the reading room of the Ritz?"

He nodded – then gestured with an open hand that she was free to go.

Reading room at the Ritz – December 16, 1916

Margaretha, dressed in her finest clothes, stepped into the reading room then paused when she saw Denvignes sitting there, waiting for her. He stood and took her white-gloved hand and kissed it as she watched his every move.

"You look divine, my dear."

"Thank you."

"Would you do me the honor of dining with me?"

Margaretha studied him carefully before she answered. "Oui." She said.

Restaurant at the Ritz

IN THE RITZ ballroom at the after-dinner dance, Margaretha, sat in the company of Colonel Denvignes.

"May I ask why you a still in Spain?" he asked. "It was my understanding you wanted to go to Holland..."

Margaretha shrugged. "I'm beginning to feel like a pawn on a chess board with no control over which move I make."

"Even when you're spending your days and nights with other men?" Denvignes asked Margaretha, taking her hand and looking at her passionately over their table.

"And why shouldn't I enjoy the offerings of Madrid in the company of a handsome uniformed man?"

"But you don't understand what it does to me - to see you dinning and dancing with other men! I... I am in love with you!"

Margaretha withdrew her hand and looked at the insecure and slightly immature man.

"I see you but once every five or six days." Margaretha told him. "When another man offers to take me to an opera or stage show, why should I not go with them?"

"You have to understand – it is my work that keeps me away. At least let me have your handkerchief as a souvenir..."

She gave him an odd look – then handed him her monogramed handkerchief. He put it to his nose and sniffed it.

"Aaahh." He said, smiling.

She sighed and leaned back in her chair. "I am waiting on instructions from Captain Ladoux. But so far I have heard nothing."

"Captain Geroge Ladoux with the Deuxième Bureau? What do you do for him?"

"I probably shouldn't tell you this," She said, leaning into him and lowering her voice, "but I am a French spy."

"Madame, I too, work for the Deuxième Bureau." He said, showing her his identification. "Anything you want to tell him - you can tell me."

Margaretha sighed in relief. "I just learned last night that the German's have several U-boats off the coast of Morocco. They are loaded with German and Turk officers and munitions. They plan to send them ashore to start an uprising."

"And from whom did you get this information?"

"The German attaché here in Madrid."

"Ah, major von Kalle." Denvignes was immediately intrigued. "If we are to foil this, we'll need more information."

"Such as..."

"Such as the exact date and time of the landing and number of people involved."

"*Then* will I get the one million francs Ladoux promised me?"

"Do you have any reason to believe you will not?"

"Actually, yes. I have not heard a word from him after he sent me here."

"Allow me to look into it. Meanwhile, get me that information from von Kalle."

December 16, 1916 - Afternoon

Tired and nearly spent, Von Kalle finally left Margaretha's hotel room late in the day. Margaretha bounded off the bed, anxious to relay the information about the submarines to Captain Ladoux. Sitting at her dressing table, she began writing down the details of her conversation with Von Kalle.

That night she triumphantly reported it to Paris.

"Now *that* must be worth the one million francs you promised me." Margaretha told Ladoux over the phone.

"We'll see."

"What do you want me to do now?"

"Sit tight and wait for my further instructions."

"But I am running out of money..."

"That is not my concern."

Margaretha hung up. Looking over at the bed, its blankets tossed about, she get's mad at herself and hurls the telephone across the room.

❖   ❖   ❖

Chapter 15

"I enjoyed the company of many men..."

❖   ❖   ❖

"FOR THE NEXT month I bounced back and forth between Denvignes and von Kalle like a tennis ball." Margaretha told Sister Leonide. "I wanted to prove that I was important – that I could be of use. So, I tried to impress Colonel Denvignes with my ability. I tossed names around like sugared almonds at a wedding. Names of people I knew – and people I wish I knew." Margaretha sighed. "I began making up stories for – and about – others. It was like a game to me."

"What happened?"

"Then a friend of mine, Senator Junoy, told me he'd been advised to break off his friendship with me..."

January 2, 1917

MARGARETHA PUSHED the door to Colonel Denvignes outer office aside with such force the glass in its window almost shattered.

"I demand an explanation!" Margaretha shouted as she marched into the room.

179

Colonel Denvignes secretary looked at her warily.

"Major – could you come in here?" the secretary asked.

Major Ernst von Damme stepped into the room from Colonel Denvignes office

"May I help you?" He asked.

"No – you may not! I am here to see Colonel Denvignes!"

"Colonel Denvignes left for Paris on business last night. Now, I ask again – may I help you?"

"Who in hell's name are you?!"

"I am Major von Damme, his temporary replacement."

"This morning, a Spanish friend of mine revealed he had been advised by a French secret agent to break off his friendship with me! And I want to know the reason why!"

"I'm sorry, I know nothing about this. You will have to talk to the Colonel himself."

"I'll just do that! I planned to return to France anyway."

With that, Margaretha turned and marched from the office leaving the major and the secretary trading questioning glances.

January 4, 1917

MARGARETHA WATCHED FROM her compartment window as the train pulled up to the platform of the Gare d'Austerlitz in Paris. Stepping out of her car she happened to see Denvignes on the platform, about to enter another car.

"Colonel Denvignes!" She shouted, running up to him as he climbed in. "I've been..."

"If you wish to talk to me," He said abruptly, cutting her short, "contact my office in Madrid."

With that, he shut the door. The train's steam whistle sounded. Stunned into silence, Margaretha could only watch as the train slowly chugged out of the station.

Checking into the Hotel Plaza Athenée – she then went to get her hair tinted, which was beginning to show more grey with each passing day. Her next stop - Captain Ladoux at the Deuxième Bureau.

January 7, 1917

Margaretha boldly marched into Captain Ladoux's office.

"It is about time!" She stated bluntly.

Ladoux, at his desk going over paperwork, barely acknowledged her intrusion. "For what?" He asked.

"For the last three days I've been here to see you, and each time I was told you were out. It was a good thing in happened to see you enter the building this morning."

Ladoux frowned. "What do you want?"

"I am here to collect my one million francs for the information I've gathered from von Kalle for Colonel Denvignes. I sent you several letters..."

"I know nothing of any letters – or about any Colonel Denvignes."

"But..."

"Now, I'm a busy man and can't be wasting my time on the likes of you. Good-day to you."

With that – the interview was over.

"What did you do?" Sister Léonide asked.

"What could I do? For the next month I went on living in Paris as if there were not a cloud in the sky. I enjoyed the company of many men in uniform. After all, there seemed to be an infinite variety of them. Then I got a pleasant surprise..."

February 3, 1917

WALKING INTO THE Hotel Plaza Athenée, Margaretha, wearing a fedora accented with a huge ostrich feather, and a fur collar coat, was pleasantly surprised to find Vadime Maslov waiting for her in the lobby.

"Vadim!" she exclaimed, running into his arms. "How did you get here?! I am so glad to see you!"

181

"And I you, Marina!" he said, embracing her. "I haven't heard from you in weeks! I got a three days' leave and flew directly to Paris to find you!"

"Oh, Vadim. I am so sorry I didn't write."

"As if in some horrible dream, I tore through the Grand Hotel, questioning staff, searching the rooms looking for you. Finally one of the maids remembered you mentioning the Plaza..."

"How could you question my love after Vittel?" She asked, leaning in close to him. "After our declarations of love to each other?"

"I was afraid – because of my surgery..."

"Vadim," She said, looking him in the eye, "I love *you*. Never forget that."

Sensing the invitation in her eyes, he leaned close and gently raising her chin, passionately kissed her.

Only after they separate did he notice the other people in the lobby now watching them.

"Marina, we must talk."

"In my room."

Entering into her room on the third floor, Margaretha pulled the hatpin from her hair and removed her fedora as Vadim entered behind her, closing the door.

"You sound so serious." She said to him. "What is wrong?"

"Yesterday, I was brought to task by my superior officer."

"What on earth for? They should be giving you medals, not chewing you out..."

"He gave me this letter." Vadim handed her an envelope. "He told me it came directly from the Russian Embassy in Paris."

Margaretha glanced at the typed missive then looked at Vadim. "I'm sorry." She said. "But I do not speak Russian."

182

"The letter warns the attaché about a liaison between one of his officers, me, and a dangerous a *venturiére* - you."

"Me?" she asked innocently. "I'm now a dangerous a *venturiére?*"

Vadim smiled slightly and nodded.

"Do you have any idea of who could have written this?"

"No – though I suspect the letter may come from my uncle, the Admiral. He's a Russian aristocrat and has never approved of you."

"I don't understand..." Margaretha said, running the events of the past few days over in her mind. "First my friend in Spain – then Colonel Denvignes and Captain Ladoux – and now you. What is going on?"

"I do not know." Vadim told her. "But I don't like it."

"Stay with me..." She pleaded. "I've been frantic with worry. Not only has Ladoux shunned me, he hasn't paid me and I am being shadowed wherever I go! Help me find out what is happening."

"Marina, I do not trust these men. It's possible one of them wrote this. My advice is to get back to the Netherlands and out of their reach as soon as possible."

"Spend the night with me..."

"I'm sorry, Marina, but I've wasted two days just looking for you. Now I must get back to the front before they list me as absent without leave."

"Then," She said, snuggling close to him, "at least let me give you a goodbye you will not soon forget..."

Margaretha turned to Sister Leonide. "Ten days later I was arrested at the Plaza Hotel. You know the rest of the story."

The Sister nodded. "Let us hope it has a happy ending."

Chapter 16

"She's a loose woman...the perfect scapegoat..."

❖   ❖   ❖

March 23, 1917

ONCE AGAIN MARGARETHA found herself at the table in the prison's dingy interrogation room. A single dim light bulb surrounded by a metal shade hung from the ceiling, leaving most of the room in heavy shadow.

Resting her head in her arms, she looked up when she heard the jangling of keys and the door to the room opened.

Investigative Magistrate of the Ministry of Justice, Captain Pierre Bouchardon, "the Grand Inquisitor" stepped into the room, followed by *sergent-greffier* Manuel Baudouin.

Bouchardon was a hard man, not known to show mercy to suspected criminals – nor did he attempt to disguise his immense hatred for "immoral" women - "man-eaters" he called them - like Margaretha.

Captain Bouchardon," she said, "could you tell Captain Ladoux that if he will give me my immediate freedom, and the permit to leave for Holland, I will give him, in a month, what he has asked to know, and what I know nothing about at present - the details of the organization of espionage in France and in Paris. That is what he wants to know.

Well, let him give me the opportunity to deal with it. I do not know about German secrets, but I *can* know them."

Both men paused at the door, looking at the woman illuminated in the pallid light of the room.

"I think Captain Ladoux may be interested." Sergeant Baudouin said, looking at the frumpy woman at the table.

Bouchardon glanced at Baudouin. "Don't be fooled Sergeant. She is used to gambling everything and anything without scruple. Without pity, she's ready to devour fortunes, leaving her lovers to blow their brains out. This woman was born to be a spy."

"Am I to be released?" Margaretha asked as they entered the room. "I know Monsieur Clunet has requested it..."

"And he very nearly succeeded." Bouchardon told her. "That is, until Captain Ladoux produced the text of the telegrams he'd intercepted at the TSF station on the Eiffel Tower."

"Telegrams? I never sent any telegrams..."

"No – but the German attaché in Madrid - your lover – von Kalle, did. He sent two of them on January 13th and a third on the 23rd, in which he gave the Foreign Ministry in Berlin a complete accounting of his dealings with you, H-21, and even asked for instructions."

"What makes you think I am this 'H-21' you're talking about?"

"It was the series of details he used that enabled our investigators to trace the clues back to you. After all, you received 3,500 pesetas from von Kalle, did you not?"

"I did. It was a personal gift."

"Then why did von Kalle telegraph Berlin on the 26th to give them an account of a payment in that exact sum to H-21?"

"And before you left for Paris, did you not ask von Kalle to have five thousand francs sent to the Comptoir d'escompte in Paris?"

"Yes, but..."

"So why did he immediately report this to Berlin – specifying that the arrival of H-21 in France was imminent?!"

Margaretha shrank in her chair. "I do not know." She said simply.

April 1917

EVEN AS MARGARETHA underwent Bouchardon's continued grilling, Maslov, now part of the fifty-thousand-man Expeditionary Force Russia sent to the Western Front, took part in the battle for the capture of the fortified Brimon Mountain range.

The battle report of his actions read: "...despite the destructive fire of artillery and numerous machine guns, he led his company by personal example into a brilliant swift attack, brought his company to the point of striking the enemy with bayonets putting the enemy to flight."

April 30, 1917

"Have you heard?" Ladoux asked Bouchardon as the grand inquisitor returned to his office several days later.

"About General Nivelle's debacle at the Second Battle of the Aisne? Of course. It is all anyone is talking about."

"I still don't understand what happened. Four hundred and eighty thousand French troops assaulting the Chemins des Dames ridge - after a six-day artillery bombardment involving five thousand three hundred guns!"

"The way their ranks were decimated by machine-gun fire," Bouchardon sighed, "it seems to me the barrage only served to alert the Germans of the impending attack."

"Forty thousand casualties on the first day alone." Ladoux shook his head in disbelief.

"And it only took two hundred and seventy-one thousand troops to be slaughtered before he finally called it off."

"I hear their bodies still cover the ridge..."

"Is it any wonder nearly half the French Army on the Western Front mutinied?"

"France has been badly shaken." Bouchardon admitted. "And even though Nivelle has resigned in disgrace, defeatism still threatens us."

"I understand that at the beginning of June, the new commander, General Philippe Pétain, plans to undertake almost three thousand five hundred courts-martials."

186

Bouchardon glanced at Ladoux. "You know, having someone, say - a German spy - on whom to blame this catastrophe would be most a most convenient out for the French government..."

"I take it you have someone in mind..."

"Not only in mind – in custody."

Ladoux thought for a moment. "You mean that dancer in Saint-Lazare?"

Bouchardon nodded. "She's a loose woman, a divorcée, a citizen of a neutral country, and a courtesan... the perfect scapegoat..."

"I will make sure her importance in the war effort is duly noted and the case against her receives maximum publicity in the French press."

"If we can convict Mata Hari, it will be a big catch for the French government."

"But we must be careful. Remember, she could reveal her dalliances with several of our own high-ranking officers - including a general."

May 15, 1917

MASLOV, WOUNDED BY a shrapnel in the "right external auditory canal" (ear) ended up in the hospital in Rennes, where he remained until May 25th. It was while recovering from these injuries that Bouchardon questioned him.

Maslov lay in his hospital bed, just one of the many wounded men on the ward, at first not paying any attention to Bouchardon when he walked into the room. Maslov's suspicions were only aroused when he noticed a nurse directing the Frenchman to his bedside.

"Vladimir Maslov?" Bouchardon asked, walking up to him.

"Yes..."

"First, let me congratulate you on your great victory..."

"Is that what they're call it when a regiment loses two-thirds of its personnel in an attack?"

"Even so, you're being considered for the "George", the Croix de Guerre with a palm branch, the Order of St. Stanislaus, 3rd class, with swords and a bow, and the Order of St. Anne, 3rd class."

"So, I've been told." Maslov studied the man. "Just who are you – and of what possible interest is it of yours?"

"I am Captain Pierre Bouchardon." He said, taking a chair next to the bed. "And I believe none of these medals would be forthcoming if your superiors knew that you were about to marry a suspected German spy."

"What? What are you talking about?"

"Margaretha Zelle was placed under arrest in February."

"So that's why I haven't heard from her..."

"And we know that the week before you saw her in Paris."

"Then you know it was only for a couple of hours on one day."

"What I want to know is why you went to see her at all."

Maslov studied the man. There was something sinister about his demeanor – something that put Maslov on his guard.

"We'd had a fling. I went to Paris to break up with her – tell her it was over."

"Still, up until the time of her arrest you corresponded regularly."

"Once or twice a week. Yes."

"What did you talk about?"

"What lovers always talk about."

"Really?"

"Yes really. Listen, in the course of my relationship with Marnia, I never saw anything that was suspect and she never once asked me for or about any military information."

Bouchardon stood and looked Maslov over. "You know, she's a whore. She only cares about herself."

"Get out!" Maslov shouted, throwing his tin coffee cup at Bouchardon. "Go back to your sewers - you French pig!"

"Fine! But She's admitted to me she no longer has any interest in you!"

"Liar!"

Bouchardon stepped into the hallway, then smiled. It was obvious he wasn't going to get anything useful from Maslov. Instead of wasting time trying to get him to turn on Margaretha, Bouchardon produced several affidavits he'd hoped to convince Maslov to sign, and simply signed them himself, using Maslov's name – then left.

June 26, 1917

MARGARETHA HEARD the jingling of keys in her cell door and turned to see Sister Leonide at the doorway.
"Captain Bouchardon wishes to question you."

"Again?" Margaretha protested as she got to her feet.

"I'm sorry, my dear." The Sister told her. "But I am only following instructions."

A few minutes later she was led into the interrogation room where Captain Bouchardon and *sergent-greffier* Baudouin sat, waiting.

"I cannot *stand* this life any longer!" Margaretha cried. "For five months now, I have been locked up in this dingy cell. I cry from fear in the night. I am nearly dying of the filth, the lack of care for my body, the disgusting food they set out for me in a bowl, as if I were a dog... I would rather *hang* myself on the bars of my window than live like this!"

"The appeals from the Dutch government have come to nothing." Captain Bouchardon told her calmly.

"But I am innocent! I was a spy *for* France, not *against* it!"

"Your trial will be held at the Palace of Justice in one month, on July 24." Captain Bouchardon told her. "For the duration of the trial, you will be moved to the Dépôt at the Conciergerie, next to the Palace. Is that understood?"

"I am to appear before the court like this?"

"At the Dépôt you will be allowed to bathe and wear your own clothes.

Margaretha nodded. "Captain Bouchardon," she said, "I am especially desperate to see or hear from Vadim. Has there been any word from him? I'd like to see him before he testifies..."

His cold, fixed eyes betrayed no emotion. "Maslov will not testify on your behalf." He told her. "In fact," he said, watching the words crush her like a vise, "He admitted to me he could care less if you're convicted or not."

189

"No!" Margaretha cried. "I refuse to believe that!"

"Believe it – your filthy little one-eyed Russian boyfriend has just thrown you to the wolves!"

Bouchardon, a nasty gleam in his eye, exited the interrogation room to find Sister Leonide, grim faced, waiting for him in the corridor.

"You must be truly proud of your misogynist soul." She told him. "I hope someday she will find out you've been withholding all the letters she's written to Maslov - as well as those sent to her."

"So, I destroyed the life of this woman of ill-repute. So what? Now it is time to take it."

With that, the Great inquisitor walked away.

Sister Leonide glanced into the interrogation room to see Margaretha had collapsed upon the table, sobbing, having lapsed into a deep state of depression.

July 1917

MARGARETHA WAS SILENT during her long walk down the hallway at Saint-Lazare Prison with Sister Leonide. Coming to cell #12, they paused as the jailer fitted an iron key into the door and unlocked it.

Seeing the room is now occupied by two other women, Margaretha, puzzled, looked at Sister Soeur Leonide.

"Who are they?" Margaretha asked.

"These are your new roommates." Sister Leonide told her. "They were especially chosen to share the cell with you."

"But why?"

"So you will not be alone at night. In fact, I have been ordered to keep a constant watch over you during the day."

Sighing, Margaretha sat down on the edge of her cot. Sister Leonide stood grim faced at the cell door.

"I am required to tell you," She said, "that, as a condemned prisoner, you may avail yourself of several special privileges."

Margaretha gave her a suspicious look. "Such as..."

"You are free to smoke and have access to any reading materials you desire."

Margaretha chuckled. "And since I neither smoke, nor enjoy reading, it looks as though I will not be availing myself of *those* particular special privileges. Is there anything else?"

"Yes. Your food will be of higher quality..."

Margaretha nodded her approval.

"...and you will be able to receive visitors, letters, and flowers."

Margaretha looked at Sister Leonide. "I ask you, Sister, in all my time here, have I ever had visitors, letters, or flowers?"

The Sister shook her head. "Perhaps I shouldn't tell you this," Sister Leonide said, "but the reason you never heard from anyone is because Captain Bouchardon confiscated all your mail."

"I suspected as much. May I see it now?"

"I am truly sorry, but he keeps it under lock and key."

"So that is why the three letters I wrote were returned unopened."

The Sister nodded. "They never even left the prison."

Margaretha glanced at her roommates and shook her head.

Margaretha finally moved out of Saint-Lazare after five months, but only for a few days, and only to the Conciergerie, to be closer to the Palace of Justice. Four days later, Adjutant Riviére accompanied her across the courtyards, up the magnificent spiral staircase to the second-floor courtroom where her trial was to take place.

She no longer looked the part of a glamorous dancer. She'd lost too much weight and appeared haggard, defeated, her hair a dirty rat's nest, no makeup, her face drawn.

But she still carried herself like a dancer, supple, fluid, undulant, her back straight, her head held high.

Chapter 17

"She was born to be a spy!"

❖   ❖   ❖

July 24th, 1917

THE TRIAL OF The Republic of France vs. Marguérite Ger-
trude McLeod-Zelle began at 1:00 o'clock in the afternoon.
The Court was presided over by 54-year-old Lieutenant-
Colonel Albert Ernest Somprou (who displayed the required law books

in front of him – The Military Code of Justice, The Criminal Instruction Code, and the ordinary Penal Code,) along with government commissioner and public prosecutor, Lieutenant André Mornet, a very thin man with a large beard. The clerk of the court was Adjutant Riviére.

The jury was made up of seven military gentlemen – one unknown plus Battalion Chief Fernand Joubert, Captain Jean Chatin, Captain Lionel de Cayla, Lieutenant Henri Deguesseau, Adjutant of Artillery Berthomme, and the lowest in rank, second Lieutenant of the Seventh Regiment of Cavalry Joseph de Mercier de Malaval.

Wearing a low-cut blue dress and tri-cornered hat, Margaretha, "free and without handcuffs" was led through the various courtyards then up a spiral staircase to the second floor where she entered courtroom of the Court of Assizes.

Margaretha was led to her seat on the long side of the room, facing seven high windows looking to the north. Her defense attorney, 74-year-old Maître Édouard Clunet, a veteran international lawyer (and ex-lover) sat just below and in front of her.

At the start of the trial, the hearing was open to the public – many of whom were present at the far end of the courtroom. Reporters occupied the press box to Margaretha's left.

"Please give the court your Christian name, date and place of birth." Colonel Somprou instructed her as Adjutant Riviére wrote down her replies.

"Zelle, Marguerite Gertrude. Forty years-old. Born in Leeuwarden, Holland."

"Civil status?"

"Divorced."

"Profession?"

"Dancer."

"Address?"

"Paris, at number 12 Boulevard des Capucines."

"The Grand Hotel?" Riviére asked.

193

Margaretha nodded. She was then excused and returned to her seat.

"Colonel Somprou," Captain Bouchardon said, standing, "I ask that this hearing be closed to the public."

"On what grounds?"

"I fear the publicity might endanger the safety of the State." Bouchardon glanced at the reporters busy taking down notes. "I also request that publication of the report of the hearings be prohibited."

"Maître Clunet," Colonel Somprou said, "Your opinion as counsel for the defense?"

Clunet glanced at Margaretha and sighed - he could offer no logical argument. Reluctantly he nodded.

"Colonel Somprou?" Battalion Chief Joubert asked, getting to his feet. "The jury would like to deliberate on this question in private."

Colonel Somprou nodded and the men in the jury stood and left the room through the doors on Margaretha's right. It was then she noticed the clock on the wall above and behind where she sat, next to which was a bust of "Marianne," symbol of the French republic. To Margaretha, the eyes of Marianne were looking down upon her, already pronouncing judgement. The spell was only broken when the jury marched back into the courtroom fifteen minutes later, taking their seats on the bench.

Battalion Chief Joubert stood up. "The votes having been taken separately," He began, "and conforming to the law on each of these questions, the jury, considering that the dissemination of the hearings would endanger the public order – believing moreover, that it would be equally endanger the public order to allow publication of the report of the *Affaire Zelle* – declares unanimously that there is reason (1) to have the hearing closed to the public, and (2) to prohibit publication of the report."

"So be it." Colonel Somprou said, bringing his gavel down. He glanced at the men in the press box. "The trial will now be held behind closed doors in front of the third military council of the High Court in Paris, in accordance with article 113, paragraphs 3 and 4 of the Code of Military Justice.

194

"The proceedings shall be public on pain of being declared null and void; nevertheless, if such publicity appears to be dangerous to public order and morals, counsel orders that the proceedings shall be held in camera. In all cases, the judgement shall be pronounced in public. Counsel may prohibit the reporting of the case. Such prohibition shall not apply to the judgement."

With that, the reporters and the public were ushered out of the courtroom and its doors closed. Margaretha looked around at the empty press box and vacated seats in the space reserved for the public.

The trial opened with Margaretha's defense, Maître Clunet's opening speech alone lasting until almost 4:00 o'clock. He decided to start by questioning her service to Germany.

"Please tell us of your first meeting with Captain Ladoux."

"I was not well in Holland and I went to Paris to go to Vitol. Vitol is in the zone of the Army, and to go there you must have a special permission so I went to the police and they made my paper out and asked for my reasons, etc., and then one day I received a note from the lawyer to go to his office and saw Captain Ladoux on the second floor. He was very polite. He said "I know you very well. I have seen you dancing. There is a lady by your name in Antwerp." I told the Captain I was never in Antwerp. The last time I was in Brussels was in 1912.

"One day the captain said to me "You can do so many things for us if you like." And he looked at me in the eyes. I understood. I thought about it for a long time.

I said "I can."

He said "Would you?"

I said "I would."

"Would you ask much money?" he said.

I said: "Yes, I would."

"What would you ask?"

I said: If I give you plenty of satisfaction, I ask you [for] one million."

He said: "Go to Holland, and you will receive my instructions."

"If it is for Germany I do not like to go."

"No." he said. "It is for Belgium."

"So, I awaited his instructions in my home."

"Then you went to Spain after that?'

"Yes."

"Will you describe Captain Ladoux?

"A fat man with [a] very black beard and very black hair and spectacles."

"How tall?"

"He was tall and fat. Fatter than a man of fifty years."

"Has he any peculiarity in his speech? Any particular habits? Did he speak loudly – or softly?"

"I did not make any impression of that. He smokes all the time. He always has a little cigarette in his lips."

"Please tell the court," Clunet urged her, "about your meeting with Monsieur Kroemer."

"On or about May 10, 1916, I was home in The Hague when the doorbell rang. It was rather late and when I opened it, I found myself face to face with Monsieur Karl H. Kroemer, the German consul in Amsterdam, who had written that he would be coming to see me – but without saying why."

"Go on."

"It has come to my attention that you have requested a visa for France. Is that true?" Monsieur Kroemer asked, stepping through her front door and into the living room without being invited. Margaretha remained silent, looking him over.

"It is." She replied, shutting the door and turning to him.

"I wonder then whether you would be willing to render us some service..."

"Service? What kind of service?"

"We would like you to gather any information while you're there which you feel might interest us."

"You want me to become a spy?! For Germany?!"

"Spy is such a harsh word. There is nothing clandestine about this. I only ask you to keep your eyes and ears open during your various pursuits, and report anything interesting back to me."

"I don't know..."

"I am authorized to pay you up to twenty thousand francs..."

"I used to make twice that for just one performance. That doesn't sound like very much for what you are asking me to do."

"It's not – but in order to get more you would have to show us what you can do."

"And what was your reply?" Clunet asked her.

"I did not give him any definite answer – but asked for time to think it over. After he left, I thought of my expensive furs which the Germans had kept – and I'm told, later sold. The value of my things is at least twice twenty thousand francs - but receiving something for them was better than nothing."

"And it was on this basis that you proceeded. In your mind he wouldn't be paying you for spying – he would be compensating you for your losses."

"Exactly. Consequently, on May 14 I wrote to Kroemer. I told him: 'I have thought it over – you can bring the money. What do you want from me? I am willing to do whatever you want. I don't ask for your secrets and I don't want to know your agents."

"Why did you tell him that?"

"Because I am an international woman. I didn't want him to discuss my means and have my work spoiled by secret agents who don't understand me or my methods."

"His reply?"

"Kroemer showed up at my apartment in The Hague a week later on the 21st, handing me twenty thousand francs in new French bills."

Margaretha and Kroemer sat on her sofa. Before them is a coffee table, on which sits a tray and coffee service.

"From now on," Kroemer told her, producing three small bottles, marked 1, 2, and 3, and setting them on the table. "I want you to write me using only secret ink. There are certain inks which no one can read. All you have to do is sign your letters 'H-21' and we will know who they are from."

"Could you see what was in the bottles?" Clunet asked her.
"Yes. The first and third were filled with a transparent liquid, while the second bottle was blue-green, a bit like absinthe."
Clunet nodded.

"This is the way you proceed." Kroemer explained. As she watched he moistened a sheet of paper with number one, wrote with number two, and cleaned it all off with number three. "And then with ordinary ink you can write me a plain letter on the same sheet of paper."
"Where do I send them? To the embassy?"
"No. Address all your letters to me at the Hotel de l'Europe in Amsterdam."

"Having the twenty thousand francs in my pocket," Margaretha continued, "I bowed Monsieur Kroemer politely out of the front door – when he stopped me."

"I can't figure out why my counterpart in the German Intelligence has not recruited you for his service?" Kroemer told her at the door.
"Probably because he doesn't know me."
"If only you could arrange for that someday – but that's for later."
"You can get anything you want from me."
"First, you prove to me you're worth your salt. Once we are sure of you – you can be sure of us."
"But I considered spending the time getting to know the man just a great loss of time. After all, as long as Ladoux did not want to pay me, there was no reason for me to reveal my great secret to him and tell him what I had in mind all just for nothing."
"I can assure you that I never wrote him one single word from Paris."
"Did you want to go back to Holland via Switzerland or England?"

"England. Oh, and I should tell you, by the way, once our ship was in the canal which goes from Amsterdam to the North Sea, I dropped the three bottles in the water, having first emptied them."

"And please tell the court why," Clunet instructed, "you chose England?"

"I certainly did not look forward to the prospect of having to go via Germany – where they would ask me what I had done with the twenty thousand francs – without giving them anything in return. If – at that moment – I had had anything on my mind which might have made me suspect to the French, I certainly would have accepted the offer to go back home via Germany."

"No further questions, your hon..., I mean, sir." Clunet said, sitting down at his table.

LIEUTENANT BOUCHARDON looked through the files in his attaché case, pulling out some papers, then stood, collecting his thoughts. He then began to pace in front of the witness box asking Margaretha questions while studying the jury.

"It says here you have been under surveillance in France since June of 1916."

"Really? I didn't realize I was that popular."

"From the reports we have on you, you were most popular indeed. At the Grand Hotel you tried principally to meet officers of various nationalities who were on their way through. Thus, on the twelfth of July you had dinner with a French officer."

"Yes. That was Lieutenant Hallaure, I believe."

"On the fifteenth, sixteenth, seventeenth, and eighteenth of July you shared a room with a certain Belgian Major Beaufort. On the thirtieth of July you were in the company of a Major Jovilcevic from Montenegro. On August 3, you were seen with Second Lieutenant Gasfield and Captain de Maslov. The fourth of August you had dinner at Armenonville with Captain Mariani, an Italian."

"If that's all you've got then I'm afraid your surveillance team was not all that observant."

199

"We'll see about that. On August 16 you had dinner at the Gare de Lyon with a French staff officer, Captain Gerbaud, who was leaving for Chambéry. On August 21, you went to Aremenonville with a British officer. The twenty-second you had lunch with two Irish officers, James Plunkett and Edwin Cecil O'Brien. On the twenty-fourth you lunched with General Baumgarten. On August 31, you had lunch at Armenonville with an English officer who had arrived that morning, James Stewart Fernie."

Bouchardon tossed the paper back on his table, then turned to Margaretha.

"Without wanting to accuse your informants of anything more serious than imprudence, your daily meetings with all those officers could have supplied you, in adding two and two together, with an overall knowledge that would have been very interesting to the Germans."

Margaretha shook her head and sighed.

Bouchardon leveled his gaze at her. "You make me want to vomit – professing a great love for that gullible young Russian dupe, de Maslov. You're already the official mistress of the Dutch Colonel van der Capellan, and mistress of the Belgian commandant, the Marquis de Beaufort! You're having affairs with a Montenegrin officer, an Italian, two Irish, three or four English, and five French officers! And now you present yourself as the fiancée of Captain Vladimir Maslov? We discovered cards and letters in your room from fifty-three men! Fifty-three! I want you to know we questioned them all!"

"Fifty-three? Is that all? I could have sworn there were more..."

"Dear God, woman! Have you no shame?!"

"And what did they say about me?"

"What else would you expect from married men - embarrassed their names might appear in the newspapers and court proceedings? Of course, they all claimed you were a lovely, charming woman. None of them would admit any action on your part even hinting at espionage." He glanced at the jury. "Of course, they were covering for themselves."

"I object!" Clunet said, jumping to his feet. "Opinion."

"I withdraw the statement."

"I love officers!" Margaretha declared. "I would rather be the mistress of a poor officer than a rich banker. My greatest pleasure is to go to bed with them without thinking of money, to compare the different nationalities."

"What an absolute whore!" Bouchardon turned to the men on the jury. "At least my wife deceived me with only one lover – the only one that I found out about, anyway."

The men laughed. Bouchardon turned back to Margaretha.

Contemplating his approach, Bouchardon paced back and forth, then paused and glanced at her.

"Is it true my men only saw you in the company of men in uniform?"

"No. I've known a good number of Frenchmen outside the military as well. And quite intimately. But I admit, the uniform has always held a great fascination for me."

"I object your Honor." Clunet said, standing. "Relevance."

"I am not a judge, Monsieur Clunet." Colonel Somprou stated. "I am a military officer."

"I object, *Sir.*"

"Overruled."

"Do you really expect this court, to believe that with all those different officers you've just admitted sleeping with, you never talked about the war? Or that you had sex with only officers simply because you preferred them to civilians?"

"I expect you to believe it because it's true. I swear that the relations I have had with the officers you mention were inspired by the same feelings and sentiments that well up within every man. And moreover, those gentlemen came to see *me*. I've said yes to them with all my heart. They left thoroughly satisfied, without ever having mentioned the war, and neither did I ask them anything that was indiscreet. I kept on seeing Maslov because I adore him."

"And you expect us to believe you did absolutely nothing for the twenty thousand francs Kroemer paid you?"

"Again, Yes." She paused for a moment collecting her thoughts. "Once back in Madrid on December 8, 1916, the circumstances

201

obliged me to act along the lines which you know by now. Captain Ladoux had not paid me anything. He had abused my confidence and I had only a few hundred pesetas left. It was then I went to see von Kalle, who knew nothing about me."

"And why did you meet with him?"

"I wanted to see whether I could manage to safeguard my trip through Germany without being arrested."

"Please continue."

"So, in order to gain von Kalle's confidence – to show him I was performing my spy duties - I sought out information concerning the military."

"And where did you find this information?"

"Old Paris newspapers. It was publicly known information which was of no importance whatever and which could not do any harm to France. I also 'revealed' to him I'd received an offer to spy for the French."

"Then what happened?"

"Von Kalle cabled his superiors to ask whether he could pay me any money. I had asked for ten thousand francs - but Berlin refused. I don't know whether a later message did authorize the Military Attaché to pay me."

"It is true that von Kalle paid me three thousand five hundred pesetas, but I would guess that was his own money. He had committed some most intimate acts with me in his office and had offered me a ring. Since I don't like that kind of thing I had declined the offer, and I suppose that he gave me the three thousand five hundred pesetas instead."

"As to those two payments of five thousand francs," Margaretha explained, "perhaps that money did come from Kroemer, because before I had left Holland, I had told my maid that in case I sent her a telegram asking for money, she could go to the Hotel de l'Europe and ask for Kroemer – but only in case it was impossible to get in touch with the Baron.

"I cabled my maid in October of 1916 and had the telegram sent via the Dutch consulate. And I sent a similar telegram in January of

1917. But I doubt whether Anna had to go to Kroemer, and I believe that the money simply came from the Baron."

"And why do you believe that?"

"Because that's what she wrote me."

"We take note of your confession." Bouchardon said matter of factly.

"I object your Honor – I mean, Sir!" Clunet shouted, getting to his feet. "My client was not confessing! She was trying to convince the court of her innocence!"

"How so?"

"She freely admitted to taking the twenty thousand francs Kroemer paid her – but did absolutely no spying for the Germans. Isn't it obvious she had no intention of doing anything for some further payment later?"

"Are you saying the *purpose* for which she obtained the money for did not matter – only the fact that she did nothing for it?"

"Exactly."

"Overruled."

"But if you really did nothing for Germany after having received that money," Bouchardon continued, "you would have easily been found out by von Kalle. Answering his first telegram about you, Berlin would immediately have said that you had fooled them and that you were no good as an agent. But we have the text of all messages exchanged between von Kalle and Berlin during a whole month, and Berlin has never made any allusion to a betrayal on your part."

Margaretha collected herself.

"Because I didn't betray them. But I didn't do anything *for* them, either."

Bouchardon, pacing the courtroom floor, waved her answer off.

"You can hardly expect us to believe that Kroemer gave you twenty thousand francs without your having proved to them that you were worth that much money! Germany gives nothing for nothing! And the funds which they usually supply their agents as travel expenses are *far* below the amount you got – which can only mean one thing – you must have worked for them previously – and our reasoning is confirmed by your own statements, as made to von Kalle."

"I was given the amount they felt I deserved." Margaretha said. "As for the inner workings of German Intelligence – I make no pretense to understand it. I am a courtesan - I admit it! But a spy? Never! I have always lived for love and pleasure!"

Bouchardon paused his pacing and looked at Margaretha.

"We know from his first telegram that you were sent twice to France to spy for the Germans. You have talked about the second trip – now let's talk about the first."

Margaretha sighed.

"Lieutenant Bouchardon – one doesn't simply send a woman like me off on a trip – a woman who has a home and a lover in Holland, without supplying her with funds. And as to my first trip to France – it had nothing whatever to do with Kroemer. I told von Kalle only that I had twice *been* to France – not that I was *sent* there."

Bouchardon contemplated for a moment.

"And why did you make use of the Dutch consulate to send your maid, Anna Lintjens, your two telegrams in which you asked for money? There must have been something mysterious in those telegrams – our you would have used regular channels. Didn't you use the then consulate at other times as well? Specifically, to send information to Kroemer?!"

"I assure you that I only used the consulate for those two telegrams."

"But why?"

"Because it was quicker that way."

Bouchardon gave Clunet a wry smile as the barrister picked up a small glass jar from the evidence table.

"What I have here," Bouchardon explained, "is secret, invisible ink!" He thrust the jar in Margaretha's face. "Don't bother to deny it! It was found among *your* belongings! What do you have to say about this?!"

"Not much." Margaretha said, laughing.

"And would you mind telling the court what you find so amusing?"

"What I find amusing is *you*." She said, smiling. She took the jar in hand and held it up for everyone to see. "You can buy this at any department store in Paris. It's the body makeup I used when I danced as Mata Hari."

Annoyed, Bouchardon snatched the jar from her fingers and set it back on the evidence table with an audible clunk.

"Is it not true," He demanded, "that when interviewed by journalists you stated, and I quote "I was born in Java, in the midst of tropical vegetation, and, since my earliest childhood, priests initiated me into the deep significance of these dances which form a real religion." Unquote."

He looked her in the eyes.

"Are you not the result of a Scottish lord's indiscretion with a Malay temptress who died in childbirth?" Bouchardon studied her. "Well?"

Margaretha rolled her eyes and sighed.

"I was born in northern Holland in 1876." She said, calmly and deliberately. "My father's name was Adam Zelle. My mother was Antje van der Meulen. I have three younger brothers, Johannes Hendriks, Arie Anne, and Cornelis Coenraad. And I have never claimed anything different."

"Aha! So, you admit you lied to the journalists!" Bouchardon said triumphantly, turning to the seven men on the jury. "I ask you - what more proof do you need of her dubious and dishonest character?!"

"I didn't lie to anyone."

"Then what about all this Java nonsense?"

"You're quoting Mata Hari's fictional background – not Margaretha Zelle's."

"Where did you get this character, Mata Hari, from anyway?"

"I acquired a superficial knowledge of Indian and Javanese dances when I lived in Malaysia for several years in with my ex-husband. When I decided to dance professionally, my personal booking agent, Gabriel Astruc, suggested I do it under a different name."

"Speaking of the name Mata Hari – just where did it come from?"

Margaretha shrugged. "I made it up."

Bouchardon studied the men in the jury. No one seemed particularly interested in his line of questioning. He was losing his audience. He decided to change course.

"Why did you want to go to Vittel?" Monet asked.

Margaretha sighed. "I answered that several times during interrogation. You have the notes."

"Please tell the court."

"I went to Vittel for my health. To drink the waters – and to see my fiancée, Vadim Maslov."

"And just what was a Russian soldier doing at a French spa?"

"A section of the spa has been turned into a hospital for wounded soldiers. He was there recuperating from a mustard gas attack which had almost blinded him."

"Then you admit you lied to Monsieur Ladoux!"

"I never did!"

"Then how do you explain that when he asked you about the need for a visit to this spa you told him you planned to take the cure. Yet, at the same time you wrote to your lover in Holland, Baron van der Capellen, that you felt fine."

Margaretha waved it off. "It was a little white lie. The same kind many women use."

Bouchardon looked at her, then collected his thoughts.

"Madame Zelle," Bouchardon began, "I would like to give you a very simple exposé of what *we* are thinking. When you were talking to Monsieur Ladoux, you carefully kept your relations with Kroemer hidden – as well as the number H-21 he had given you, and the mission he had trusted you with. Is that true?"

Margaretha nodded. "Yes."

"On the other hand, when you were first talking to von Kalle, your first move was to tell him that you had *acted* as if you had accepted a mission from the French. Now whom did you serve under those circumstances? Whom did you betray Madame Zelle? France or Germany?!"

Margaretha looked at him for a moment before she spoke. "If my attitude towards the Germans and the French was different," she explained, "it was because I wanted to hurt the first – a plan in which I succeeded – and help the second – a plan which was equally successful. After all, I couldn't expect to get permission to travel through Germany for selling them a bottle of vinegar! I was obviously obliged to make them believe that I was on their side – while in reality the French were leading the game. Once I had obtained certain information from von Kalle, I tried to see Captain Ladoux three times on the Boulevard Saint Germain."

"And had you been able to see him, what would you have told him?"

"I would have given him the information I learned and said 'Here is a free sample of what I am able do. Now it's your turn.'"

"There is another explanation for your actions, you know."

"Oh?"

"It was impossible for you to visit von Kalle without being seen by one of our agents. You therefore simply *had* to make your preparations so as be able to say to us 'I am going to see von Kalle – but I am doing it for *you!*'"

"What? How can you say that?"

"Anyone who is familiar with espionage knows that whenever a German agent finds himself in a situation like yours, the enemy always supplies him with certain information in order to gain our confidence – but while that information is true, it has lost its value by the time he tells us about it."

Margaretha became indignant. "I assure you," She told Bouchardon, "that your way of thinking is worth absolutely nothing. I had never done any espionage before meeting Kroemer. I have always lived for love and for pleasure. I have never purposely associated with people who could give me information – nor have in tried to find access to certain important circles."

"And let me point out to you, sir, that the information I got from von Kalle was neither old, nor unimportant! Colonel Denvignes told me that General Goubet found it most interesting."

"You just said that you knew nothing about espionage."

"I did. I mean, I don't. I mean, yes I said that – and no I don't know anything about spying."

"That ties in very badly with those great secret plans of yours for which you wanted a million francs."

"I had only mentioned to the Germans people I knew in France – but I would have been able to build up connections in Belgium, which, under Captain Ladoux's guidance, would have led to great things. And besides, the whole idea of becoming a spy - and the plan to spy for both countries simultaneously - was all Captain Ladoux's idea – not mine."

"About those officers..."

"I am not a woman that kisses and tells."

"Please. You've been practicing horizontal espionage and collecting confessions on the pillow for years!" Bouchardon turned to the court. "I ask you - with a moral character like that, how could she *not* be a spy?"

"I would like to call Captain Ladoux back to the stand." Clunet said.

MARGARETHA STEPPED down as she and the captain traded places in the witness box. Clunet stepped over to the evidence table, picked up a handful of transcribed papers, paused and looked at Captain Ladoux.

"What actual proof do you have that this woman is a spy?" Édouard Clunet asked Captain George Ladoux.

"Those transcripts of the incriminating radio traffic are the proof. I personally intercepted them between her and Germany. As you can see, one of the messages, concerning the accession to the Greek throne of the Heir Apparent, Prince Georges, mentions that 'agent H-21 has proved very useful.'"

"And you believe Margaretha Zelle-McLeod to be this German Agent H-21?"

"Yes."

"And exactly what information did she reveal to the Germans?"

Ladoux, caught off-guard by the question, was silent.

"To reveal that information is impossible."

"Why?"

"There is material within them that threatens our national security and because of which, I have omitted it from the transcripts."

"Your honor..."

"Monsieur Clunet, I am not a judge. I am an officer."

"Sir, I object.

"Over-ruled. France is at war with Germany. For reasons of national security, you cannot be allowed access to the recordings. And you are denied permission either to cross-examine the prosecution's witnesses or to examine your own witnesses directly."

"Is it not true, Captain, that even as my client was writing her letter in her hotel room that night, Major von Kalle, back at the German embassy, was transmitting a radio message to Berlin?"

"The timing sounds correct."

"And that, unknown to Major von Kalle, you, sitting in your tiny room atop the Eiffel Tower, were listening and recording the transmission the entire time?"

"That is true."

"Is this the transcription of that message?"

"It is."

"In general terms for the court, what did the message say?"

"In it, Major von Kalle described the helpful activities of a German spy, code-named H-21, stating, and I quote:

"Agent H-21 has been engaged by French but was returned to Spain by British and now asks for money and instructions."

"Is that all?"

"The message also stated that this spy belonged to the Cologne Center of Espionage and had been sent to France for the first time in March..."

"At which time my client was still in Holland..."

"If you say so."

"Go on."

"It went on to say H-21 told the German chief of espionage about the preparation for the Allied general offensive in the spring of 1917. Von Kalle also transmitted that H-21 had taken the *Hollandia* from

209

Spain to England on a mission for the French and had been returned by the British."

"So," Monsieur Clunet said to Captain Ladoux, "now you had all the evidence you needed to arrest her."

Ladoux nodded.

Monsieur Clunet gave Ladoux a tired look.

"Honestly, Captain, do you expect this court to believe this transcription, which reads more like those found in dime-novels than like any cryptic coded telegrams *I've* ever read, and the information it contains, which it has been revealed actually came from old French newspapers, is evidence?" Clunet turned to the jury. "Anyone reading this text would conclude only *one* person was being discussed – Margaretha Zelle! In fact, the only thing that seems to be missing in these "transcripts" is her full name and date of birth!"

"I cannot be held responsible for what General Walter Nicolai, the German chief Intelligence Officer ordered transmitted." Ladoux explained.

"And just why would he have ordered von Kalle to send such an erroneous message?"

"Don't you understand? The German Army had grown very annoyed that she was only providing him with mere Paris gossip about the sex lives of French politicians and generals."

"Are you saying General Nicolai decided to terminate her employment by exposing her as a German spy to the French?"

"Yes. Exactly."

Clunet became indignant. "Then how do we know she passed on any information at all? These are just words on paper! Anyone could have made this up. No – if you are going to introduce radio messages as evidence, I insist on hearing the unedited recordings myself to verify their accuracy."

"For one thing, she admitted taking German money." Captain Ladoux continued. "Why would they pay her if she were not spying for them?"

"She told the court why!"

210

"Secondly, she had the code name H-21. Although I must admit seeing the H had me baffled..."

"Oh? Why is that?"

"I've never seen an H call letter used by the Germans before. I first I thought it might have been some pre-war designation."

"Might it not be possible," Clunet offered, "that the Germans themselves threw French intelligence on a false track? That they are telegraphing only what they want you to know?"

Ladoux waved the suggestion off. "I doubt seriously if that is possible."

"Your honor," Clunet pleaded, "I mean, Sir, Captain Ladoux is the only person to have ever heard the original fourteen messages prior to their decoding and translation. I speak German fluently. I beg the court to allow me to hear the actual recorded transmissions."

"Well, Captain Ladoux?"

"I am sorry." He said, squirming in his seat. "But that is not possible."

"And why not?" Bouchardon asked. "The court is also interested in hearing the original recordings."

"I, um – I cannot find them."

"So, you're telling the court," Clunet said, "the original recordings, the one's on which you claim are evidence against my client - have now mysteriously disappeared?"

Captain Ladoux nodded.

"How convenient for France." Clunet said, giving him a disgusted look. "And for you, Captain Ladoux. Does no one else find it suspicious that Captain Ladoux was the *only* person to have listened to the original messages prior to decoding and translating them - the same messages you say cannot be found!" He turned to the court. "I ask for an immediate dismissal of all charges due to lack of evidence."

"Denied."

"So, you're willing to sacrifice this innocent woman to cover for the ineptness of France's military commanders! Let her take the blame for the disaster at the front with a concocted tale about her revealing secrets

211

of France's new tanks to German officers, which supposedly allowed them to win! I wonder how the newspapers will feel about the story..."

"In order not to hinder the investigation of cases," Bouchardon told him, "the newspapers have been ordered to keep silent about the arrest of persons suspected of espionage and war smuggling."

"Meaning?"

"The publicity given to the details of this affair is detrimental to the execution of the service of C.E. But, unless the military justice system gives a reasoned opinion to the contrary, sentences may be allowed to be published."

Clunet glanced at Margaretha and breathed a heavy sigh.

"I object, Sir!" Clunet said, standing. "Captain Bouchardon has made no distinction between her society life, which he judges to be immoral, her suspicious cosmopolitanism, or her intelligence activities. And now he's calling for her to voice an opinion."

"Over ruled."

"So, what else is new?" Clunet responded, sitting down.

Adjutant Riviére stood up. "Colonel Joseph-Cyrille Denvignes, chief of the Intelligence Section of the French embassy in Madrid is now called to the stand."

Captain Ladoux and Colonel Denvignes traded looks as they traded places on the witness stand.

"Now, Colonel," Bouchardon said, "how did you meet the defendant?"

"I first met Madame Zelle when she was in the company of an attaché of the Netherlands at the Palace Hotel - then again at a later date with a different attaché at the Ritz."

"Is that all?"

"No. I found her attractive and intriguing – so I asked her to lunch, which she accepted."

"And what took place at that luncheon?"

Colonel Denvignes, standing in the witness stand, glanced at Margaretha. Although he tried not to display it, his amorous feelings for her

212

began to stir his soul once again. He quickly frowned and gave Margaretha a disgusted look.

"I saw through her from the beginning," He stated to the court, "right from the *first moment* she came to see me."

Clunet and Margaretha exchanged glances and she shook her head.

"At some point during the conversation she mentioned the names of the Crown Prince and the Duke of Cumberland."

"The son of the Kaiser?" Bouchardon asked.

Denvignes nodded. "This proved to me that she was a spy for Germany."

"What did you do then?"

"I told her about the German submarines off Morocco and asked her to return to von Kalle to get more information."

"But that's not true!" Margaretha said to Clunet in hushed tones. He motioned her to silence.

Clunet nodded.

"And it was not Monsieur Denvignes who asked me to get him information on the landing in Morocco – he knew nothing about that! On the contrary – when I gave that information, he was perplexed by it! So much so, that on the following morning he came back to ask whether I could get more details."

"The Colonel forgets to say that he has been running after me to the extent of making himself ridiculous! Twice a day he came chasing me at the Ritz, having tea or coffee with me in front of everyone! I noticed he didn't tell you that he proposed that I come up and live with him, because I would cheer up his home. When he asked me to be his mistress, I told him that I belonged to a Russian officer, whom I was going to marry."

She looked at Denvignes.

"I am now convinced that it was the *Colonel*, knowing Maslov was my lover, that it was *he* who was behind the letter which the Russian Attaché wrote to the Colonel of the First Russian Imperial Regiment!"

"Speaking of Vadime de Maslov," Bouchardon said, standing, "I have his personal written statement here that I would like to read to the court."

"Go ahead, Captain."

"I, Vadime de Maslov, declare my affair with Margaretha Zelle was a trifling thing, and has not been of any importance. When I went to see her in March to announce a clean break with her, I found that she was in jail so could not do so."

"Do you have anything to say in response to that?"

"Until I hear the words come directly from Vadim's lips - I have nothing to say about such obvious trickery."

"In my opinion," Colonel Denvignes continued, "she didn't amount to much. She was only after the people's money."

"Thank you, Colonel Denvignes. You are excused." Bouchardon turned and looked at Margaretha. "I call Margaretha McLeod-Zelle to the stand."

She stood, adjusted her clothing, then waiting for Denvignes to sit down, took the witness stand. Clunet stood to question her.

"Do you have anything to say about Colonel Denvignes' statements?"

"I would first like to state," Margaretha began, "that *he* asked to be introduced to *me*. If he claims Mr. de With, the Attaché at the Dutch Legation, had told him my name was Mrs. McLeod, then I would like to point out that everybody in Madrid, where I have danced, knows that Mrs. McLeod and Mata Hari are one and the same person."

She caught Denvignes' eye.

"The Colonel also cleverly twists the nature of our relationship."

"I object!" Bouchardon said.

"Objection overruled."

"Go on, Mrs. McLeod." Clunet urged. "What did take place between you and Colonel Denvignes?"

"The next day around 2:30 p.m. Monsieur Denvignes was sitting in the reading room of the Ritz, knowing that I usually went there around that time."

Reading room at the Ritz - Madrid - December 1916

214

MARGARETHA, DRESSED in her finest clothes, stepped into the reading room then paused when she saw Denvignes sitting there, waiting for her. He stood and took her white-gloved hand and kissed it as she watched his every move.

"Guess whom I've come for?" He asked.

"Maybe for me?"

"You look divine, my dear."

"Thank you."

"Would you do me the honor of dining with me?"

Margaretha studied him carefully before she answered. "Oui." She said.

"And I did mention the Crown Prince and his brother-in-law, the Duke of Cumberland – but only to say that the prince has a stupid smile and that he is constantly at odds with the duke – whom I know very well and whom I can see whenever I want."

"How did you meet him in the first place?"

"It was when I was the mistress of von Kiepert, and he frequently came to dinner at my apartment."

Restaurant at the Ritz –December 1916

IN THE RITZ ballroom at the after-dinner dance, Margaretha, in the company of Monsieur de With and Monsieur Van Aersen, sat by herself as the two attachés danced with other women – when Colonel Denvignes walked into the room. Walking over to her table he sat down.

"What are you still doing in Spain?" he asked. "Why haven't you gone directly to Holland?"

"Listen – I am on your side."

"Forgive me, my darling," Denvignes said to Margaretha, taking her hand and looking at her passionately over their table, "but I've been told you've been spending your days and nights with other men..."

"And why shouldn't I enjoy the offerings of Madrid in the company of a handsome uniformed man?"

"But you don't understand what it does to me - to see you dinning and dancing with other men! I... I am in love with you!"

Margaretha withdrew her hand and looked at the insecure and slightly immature man.

"I see you but once every five or six days." Margaretha told him. "When another man offers to take me to an opera or stage show, why should I not go with them?"

"You have to understand – it is my work that keeps me away. At least let me have your handkerchief as a souvenir..."

She gave him an odd look – then handed him her monogramed hand-kerchief. He put it to his nose and sniffed it.

"Aaahh." He said, smiling.

She sighed and leaned back in her chair. "I am waiting on instructions from Captain Ladoux. But so far I have heard nothing."

"Captain Geroge Ladoux with the Deuxième Bureau? What do you do for him?"

"I probably shouldn't tell you this," She said, leaning into him and lowering her voice, "but I am a French spy."

"Madame, I too, work for the Deuxième Bureau." He said, showing her his identification. "Anything you want to tell him - you can tell me."

Margaretha sighed in relief. "I just learned last night that the German's have several U-boats off the coast of Morocco. They are loaded with German and Turk officers and munitions. They plan to send them ashore to start an uprising."

"And from whom did you get this information?"

"The German attaché here in Madrid."

"Ah, major von Kalle." Denvignes was immediately intrigued. "If we are to foil this, we'll need more information."

"Such as..."

"Such as the exact date and time of the landing and number of people involved."

"*Then* will I get the one million francs Ladoux promised me?"

"Do you have any reason to believe you will not?"

"Actually, yes. I have not heard a word from him after he sent me here."

"Allow me to look into it. Meanwhile, get me that information from von Kalle."

Bouchardon stood as Clunet sat down, and paraded back and forth in front of the jury as he talked.

"Among the exhibits seized from the dancer's hotel room, for example, is a tube containing mercury bi-iodide and potassium iodide." He glanced at Margaretha. "And if you wouldn't mind telling the court – what do you use this for?"

"When men refuse to wear one – I use it as a chemical condom." She told the court matter of factly.

"Really? The same chemicals which can be used as a developer for a secret ink? How interesting. How about the Spanish tablets of mercury oxy-cyanide?"

"It's an antiseptic. I have a prescription for it in France."

"So, you're asking the court to believe you did not know that once diluted, the tablets constitute a sympathetic ink that is safe from routine investigations?"

"No. Not until you just told me."

Bouchardon, having already decided her guilt, turned and faced the seven men in the jury, "I had the intuition that I was in the presence of a person in the pay of our enemies." His eyes narrowed as he studied Margaretha. "She has sold secrets to the Germans and reported to the French nothing but disinformation. The deaths of fifty-thousand French soldiers weighs upon her shoulders! Without scruples, accustomed to making use of men, she is the type of woman who is born to be a spy!"

"A harlot? Yes – I admit it." Said she, jumping to her feet. "But a traitoress? Never!"

Margaretha sat back down, dumbfounded.

At 7:00 that evening a recess was called until the following morning at 8:30.

Back in lock-up, Margaretha tried to bargain for her release, turning to Sister Leonide.

"Please tell Captain Bouchardon, that if Captain Ladoux can get me to give me my immediate freedom, and the permit to leave for Holland, I will give him in a month what he has asked to know, and what I know nothing about at present: the details of the organization of espionage in France and in Paris. That is what he wants to know. Well, let him give me the opportunity to deal with it. I do not know about German secrets, but I *can* know about them."

The offer was delivered but fell on deaf ears. Her fate had already been decided.

Chapter 18

"She was born to be a spy!"

❖ ❖ ❖

July 25th, 1917

THIS DAY THE indictment and closing arguments took place. When t 54-year-old Lieutenant-Colonel Albert Ernest Somprou, who presided over the Court, sat with his hands clasped behind the law books stacked in front of him.

"She not only killed fifty thousand Frenchmen," Bouchardon exclaimed, "she stole them from their wives and led a life of breathtaking extravagance while ordinary people went without bread! The evil that this woman has done is unbelievable! This is perhaps the greatest woman spy of the century!"

Clunet then spoke up.

"Bouchardon has accepted a case he knew was false." Clunet told the Jury. "He accuses my client of killing fifty thousand Frenchmen! But it is a figure he pulled out of the thin air! He's provided no actual evidence to show what she did or how it resulted."

"Her defense is to speak the truth. Though she is not French, she has the right to have friends in other countries – even those at war with France! But she remains neutral. She counts on the good hearts of French officers."

"If it please the court," Clunet said, standing, "I have yet to hear from French Minister of War, Alfred Messimy. He's been summon to appear on my client's behalf."

"About that," Somprou said, producing an envelope, "I received this letter from Madame Andrée Messimy yesterday." He opened the envelope and removed the single folded sheet of paper and began to read.

"To Alfred-Ernest Semprou, president of the tribunal.

My husband, Alfred Messimy, French Minister of War, is too ill with rheumatism at this time to appear in court. Furthermore, I hereby categorically deny and avow that he has never met the woman "Mata Hari" in his life."

"And as you can see," Semprou said, holding out the letter, it is signed: Andrée Messimy née Bonaparte."

Semprou turned his head to the jury.

"I would like to remind the jury," He began, "that it is the following eight questions on which you have to pronounce judgement.

"One, the afore-mentioned Zelle, Marguerite Gertrude, divorced wife of McLeod, called Mata Hari – Is she guilty of having entered the entrenched camp of Paris in December 1915 – or in any case within the period of the statute of limitations – to obtain documents or information in the interests of Germany, an enemy power?

"Two. Is she guilty - while in Holland during the first six months of 1916 - or in any case within the period of the statute of limitations – of having delivered to Germany, an enemy power, and notably to the person of Consul Kramer, documents or information susceptible to damage the operations of the army? Or to endanger the safety of places, posts, or other military establishments?

"Three. Is she guilty – in Holland in May 1916 - or in any case within the period of the statute of limitations – of having maintained intelligence with Germany, an enemy power, in the person of the afore-mentioned Kroemer – in order to facilitate the projected task of the enemy?

"Four. Is she guilty – of having entered the entrenched camp of Paris in June 1916 - or in any case within the period of the statute of limitations – to obtain documents or information in the interest of Germany, an enemy power?

"Five. Is she guilty – in Paris since May 1916 - or in any case within the period of the statute of limitations – of having maintained intelligence with Germany, enemy power, in order to facilitate the projected task of said enemy?

"Six. Is she guilty – in Madrid, Spain, in December 1916 - or in any case within the period of the statute of limitations – of having maintained intelligence with Germany, enemy power, in the person of the Military Attaché von Kalle in order to facilitate the projected task of said enemy?

"Seven. Is she guilty – under the same circumstances of time and place, of having delivered to Germany, enemy power, in the person of said von Kalle, documents susceptible of damaging the operations of the army or to endanger the safety of places, posts, or other military establishments, said documents or information dealing in particular with interior politics, the spring offensive, the discovery by the French of the secret of a German invisible ink, and the disclosure of the name of an agent in the service of England?

"Eight. Is she guilty – in Paris in January 1917- or in any case within the period of the statute of limitations – of having maintained intelligence with Germany, enemy power, in order to facilitate the projected task of said enemy?"

With the gaudy pomp and fanfare of the court scene in a cheap opera, after only forty-five minutes of deliberation the tribunal returned.

"Today, the 25th of July 1917, the Third Permanent Council of War in Paris had declared Zelle, Margaretha Geertruida, called Mata Hari, divorcée of Mr. McLeod, guilty of espionage and intelligence with the enemy. In consequence, the aforementioned Council condemns her to the pain of death."

"C'est impossible!" Margaretha exclaimed.

"She is innocent!" Clunet said, jumping to his feet. "And I submit that she should be acquitted!"

"Order in the court!" Alfred-Ernest Semprou shouted, slamming down his gavel. "orderly – remand the prisoner back to Saint-Lazare."

Chapter 19

"The hour of expiation has arrived."

❖   ❖   ❖

ON AUGUST 6, 1917, while Margaretha waited to hear about her appeal to the Supreme Court, the War Department's "Press Section" responded to the counter-espionage complaints:

"It is difficult, in practice, to get the newspapers, even with advance notice, to remain completely silent on matters of espionage and counter-espionage, especially when a conviction has been handed down, as was the case with the Zelle woman, known as Mata Hari."

The Paris newspapers, in fact, went wild, a blood frenzy, describing her as "a sinister Salomé who played with the heads of our soldiers in front of the German Herod." Yet the censors were particularly attentive: one of them wrote: "Mata Hari: the sound of her execution is heard periodically; we've heard it more than ten times."

August 7, 1917

Margaretha wrote several letters to the Dutch Ambassador in Paris, claiming her innocence. "My international connections are due of my

223

work as a dancer, nothing else .... Because I really did not spy, it is terrible that I cannot defend myself."

She spent her 41st birthday in the dreary filth of Saint-Lazare while her appeals were shot down one after the other like so many children's boats in a tub, starting with the Dutch Ambassador's request that her punishment be reduced to a prison sentence.

On September 27, the Supreme Court of Appeals upheld the denial. She wrote the Dutch legatee in Paris, begging him to intervene, request a presidential pardon.

As her attorney, Clunet consulted with the Dutch envoy, and a request for clemency came from The Hague "for reasons of humanity."

The French government's answer to all appeals was that the evidence against her was so overwhelming that Poincaré refused a presidential pardon.

Mr. A. J. Kooij wrote to Margaretha during this time, hoping to secure the rights to publish her memoirs and "make myself a tidy little fortune." He was sure people all over Europe would be climbing over each other to get a copy. He just knew she must be working on her memoirs – what else did she have to do besides make her hopeless appeals?

Not knowing where to write her, he addressed the letter "a Vincennes" – the execution ground. He never received a reply.

Edouard Clunet received President of the Republic, Raymond Poincaré's rejection on October 13. The order for her execution was signed the next day. Frantic, Clunet even suggested Margaretha claim to be pregnant by him – but she refused.

October 15, 1917

AT PRECISELY 5:00 a.m. that pre-dawn autumn morning, the jailer's keys rattled in the lock on the iron door to 41 year-old Margaretha's cell. Opening it, senior military officer, Captain

224

Thibaut, Pastor Arbaux, accompanied by two sisters of charity, Sister Léonide, and Sister Marie, Captain Bouchardon, and Maitre Clunet, entered the small room. Pastor Arbaux paused for a moment and looked at the still sleeping figure.

"It is remarkable." He said. "It is the last sunrise she will ever see – yet she slumbers in such a calm, untroubled sleep."

Sister Léonide woke Margaretha with a gentle shake.

"Zelle, have courage." Sister Leonide said as Margaretha blinked awake. "The president of the Republic has rejected your appeal. The hour of expiation has arrived."

"Have no fear, Sister." Margaretha said as she sat up. "I will approach death without faltering. You will see a good death."

Captain Thibaut stepped forward with a paper in hand.

"I see the official delegation has arrived." Margaretha said, catching his eye.

"I am required to ask you one final time." He said, holding out the paper. "Will you sign this full confession?"

"And I will answer you one final time." She replied, pushing it back to him. "No. For any sins which I may have committed have already been confessed to."

Seated at the edge of the bed, The sisters helped Margaretha pull on her long black, silken stockings.

"Are there any last requests my dear?" Pastor Arbaux asked.

"Just one. Will you please baptize me?"

"It would be my honor." Arbaux said. He then performed the necessary ceremony, baptizing Margaretha Zelle into the Protestant religion.

"Anything else?" Captain Thibaut asked.

"May I write three farewell letters?" She looked directly at Captain Bouchardon. "And this time have them delivered?"

Captain Thibaut gave a questioning glance at Captain Bouchardon, who, somewhat embarrassed, nodded his head. Turning to the jailer who stood outside the door, he said "See to it at once."

The jailer nodded then departed to get the writing materials.

While she waited, Margaretha pulled on her shoes. She had just finished buttoning them when the jailer returned with a pen, ink, paper, and three envelopes.

Using the seat of the black leather chair in her cell as a table top, she sat on her cot and quickly penned two letters. Finishing ten minutes later, Margaretha folded them and inserted them into the envelopes, handing them over to the custody of her lawyer.

"It is time." Captain Bouchardon told her.

Margaretha nodded, then arose and slipped a heavy silk kimono on over her nightdress. Taking her long black velvet cloak edged around the bottom with fur, from a hook over the head of her bed, she pulled it on over the kimono. Buttoning it and fastening a black belt around it, she put on her black felt hat.

"I am ready." Margaretha said, calmly pulling on a pair of black kid gloves.

Standing, Margaretha, accompanied by Sister Soeur Léonide, and Pastor Arbaux, the party slowly filed out of her cell, their footsteps echoing off the stone floor and down the long quiet hallway lined with heavy iron doors.

Exiting the building, they descended to the prison courtyard. Margaretha noticed the pavement was still wet with the rain from the night before. Now the clouds were clearing, but the sun not yet fully up as she was quickly ushered into a waiting automobile.

Captain Bouchardon, Captain Thibaut, and her lawyer Maitre Clunet entered the car after her. Father Arbaux, accompanied by the two sisters of charity followed in a second vehicle.

The cars sped through the heart of Paris, splashing through the puddles on the rain soaked streets of the city. Watching the blur of passing buildings out a side window, Margaretha was silent and reflective. Never once before had her iron will failed her. But now, alone and without friends or family, she finally came to terms with her fate. Frumpy and overweight, even her career as a dancer was nothing more than a memory. Now, life itself, it seemed, was against her.

At half-past five the vehicles turned into the Château de Vincennes, an old fort on the city's outskirts. The automobile came to a stop just past the barracks next to the firing squad, ready for the execution. The doctor of the Paris Police Headquarters stood by, bag in hand, to verify her death.

As Margaretha exited the car she composed herself, and glanced at the twelve Zouaves in their khaki uniforms and red fezzes standing shoulder to shoulder at attention, their rifles standing smartly at their sides.

Grim faced, the Zouaves commanding officer, a Sergeant-Major of the 23rd Dragoons in his navy blue uniform, watched Margaretha silently as she took a deep breath then walked unaided to a large wooden post set into the ground in front of an eight foot high hill of earth. There, she was bound to the post with a single strand of rope tied about her waist.

Father Arbaux and Monsieur Clunet walked up to Margaretha and spoke to her for a few moments. Then the Sergeant-Major approached, carrying a white cloth.

"A blindfold?" He offered.

Margaretha glanced at the piece of cloth, then looked at Clunet.

"*Must* I wear that?"

Clunet gave the Sergeant Major a questioning glance.

"If Madame prefers not, it makes no difference." Said the officer. Turning away, he walked back over to his men and drew his sword. He gestured to Father Arbaux and Clunet.

"May God bless you, child." The Father said. Both men then stepped away from her.

Margaretha collected herself, drew herself up to her full height and stood ready and waiting.

The Sergeant Major raised his sword, the dawning sun reflecting off the polished steel blade. Normally, of the twelve guns used in this type of situation, eleven contain blanks. However, he knew rumors were already circulating that his men were going to fire blanks and allow Margaretha to escape, therefore he reversed the order, with only one rifle having a blank cartridge. All the rifles had been loaded by him, and issued to the firing squad as they assembled that morning.

"Shoulder arms!" he commanded.

The rifles of the twelve men were snapped into firing position at their shoulders. For a tense moment each man stood aiming down the barrel of his gun at the heart of the women.

Margaretha then blew a kiss to her executioners.

"Fire!"

The volley rang out. Margaretha collapsed to her knees. Then one of the men in the firing squad fainted.

The other men lowered their arms as the Sergeant Major, under orders, removed his pistol from his holster and walked up to Margaretha's limply hanging body, her legs doubled up beneath her.

Standing next to her motionless body he aimed directly at her heart and pulled the trigger. Her body jerked upon the impact, but otherwise showed no signs of life.

"By God!" The Sergeant Major remarked, holstering his pistol, "This lady knows how to die."

Father Arbaux and Bouchardon looked on as Margaretha's lifeless body was removed from the firing post.

"Such a shame." The Father said, shaking his head.

Bouchardon looked at him. "Even innocent, Father, she *had* to disappear." He said coldly, turning and walking away.

"I agree." The doctor added. "She was a rascal, we did well to get rid of her."

"But why do you say that?" Father Arbaux asked.

"Because death keeps her from taking any new victims from the world." The doctor said, leveling his gaze at her body. "At the very least it put an end to the execrable career of this devious and cruel woman."

With that, the doctor turned and followed Bouchardon back to their waiting car.

Father Arbaux just looked at the men and shook his head. Kneeling down next to Margaretha he began giving her Last Rights.

October 19, 1917

VADIM MASLOV STOOD in the window of room, his fists clenched, his face twisted in a frustrated rage – and tears streaming down his cheeks. The trigger for the emotions lay open on his cot – a French newspaper – its headline: "German Spy Mata Hari Executed by Firing Squad."

Helpless to intercede, lied to (and about) by the French government, he had heard nothing from Margaretha since her arrest five months earlier. The claims that he had renounced and no longer cared for the woman he actually loved had all been manufactured by Bouchardon and others to demoralize Margaretha - the affidavits he supposedly signed, disappearing immediately after the farce of a trial.

Angry that his failing sight had ruined his career as a pilot, sick at heart, and sick of the government interference that led to Margaretha's execution, Vadim became belligerent to the men in his command, and began openly criticizing military policy. When he started to denounce the soldiers in his own company, Lieutenant E. Rapp made a report to the military commissar of the Provisional Government, stating:

"Desiring to be loyal to you, Mr. Commissar, as a representative of Russian Democracy, we, the soldiers of the 1st consolidated company of the 1st regiment, report that our company commander Headquarters, Mr. Maslov, in order to undermine your authority and cause confusion among the soldiers, openly called you and General M.I. Zankevich "bastards.""

By the end of November 1917, the situation had become so intolerable that by order of General Zankevich, the military representative of the Provisional Government in France, Maslov, once a celebrated hero, was demoted to lieutenant and removed from his post "as not corresponding to his appointment."

MARGARETHA'S DAUGHTER, Nonnie, learned of her mother's execution through the Dutch newspapers, which, like the majority of European newspapers at the time, hailed the "unmasking" of the passionate courtesan spy and considered her execution a great success. Her personal feelings about her mother are unknown. What is known is that her father refused to speak to her about Margaretha.

On August 10th, 1918, Nonnie, now 21 years-old, was about to leave for the Dutch East Indies as a teacher - when she suddenly suffered a cerebral hemorrhage, passing away almost instantly. The cause is believed to be a side effect of the syphilis Margaretha acquired from John which had been transmitted to Nonnie's growing fetus.

The censorship services banned any photographs from being taken during the execution of the dancer. The action wasn't entirely successful. Buried within the pages of *The New York Times*, Margaretha's execution merited a scant two paragraphs, labeling her "a woman of great attractiveness with a romantic history."

❖   ❖   ❖

Epilogue

"Please don't think that I'm bad."

❖   ❖   ❖

Eleven bullets had struck Margaretha. It was now determined only the pistol shot through her heart had been fatal.

FOUR DAYS AFTER Margaretha's execution, even as the French state was busy auctioning off her possessions to pay off the cost of the trial, both Georges Ladoux and Major-General Denvignes were arrested on charges of espionage for Germany.

The truth behind their persecution of Margaretha was finally revealed (shifting the blame of *their* spying onto *her* shoulders.) To save face over the murder of an innocent woman, the French government decided "it was best for all" to simply cover up the "regrettable error."

Both men were ultimately released quietly (for reasons never explained to the public) and the records of her trial sealed for the next one hundred years.

❖　　　❖　　　❖

HAVING BEEN THROUGHLY demonized by the press, Margaretha's body was never claimed by any family members. Records dating from 1918 show that the Museum of Anatomy in Paris was the final recipient. Once one of the most desirable women in Europe, Margaretha was reduced to having her head cut off and embalmed, while her torso was heartlessly cut up as practice material for medical students. When finished with, it was incinerated with the other medical waste.

According to curator of the Museum, Roger Saban, archivists discovered in 2000 that her embalmed head had disappeared, possibly as early as 1954 when the museum had been relocated. Fortunately, the ghoulish trophy has never turned up.

❖　　　❖　　　❖

UNTIL 2017, biographers' only access to Gretha's writing has been the interrogation transcripts leading up to her trial and her prison letters held in the French archives. The sealed trial and other related documents, a total of 1,275 pages, were only declassified by the French Army one hundred years after her execution.

The British Archives prove that Margaretha *never* gave the Germans any crucial information. In 1930, the German government completely exonerated Mata Hari of any and all charges of spying. But the nation that executed her, to this day shows great reluctance to even revisit her story.

A new collection of Margaretha's personal letters, *Don't Think That I'm Bad: Margaretha Zelle Before Mata Hari* (1902-1904), Edited by Lourens Oldersma (published in Dutch in 2017) reveal the hitherto unseen maternal side of her character. They chronicle her struggle to establish a new life with her daughter after leaving an abusive marriage.

232

"The letters make her much more human," says Yves Rocourt, curator of the exhibition. "You've got to admire her for continuing to rebuild her life after it crashes down. Her ability to overcome tragedy and to reinvent herself, a very modern concept, is central to understanding her character. She's a strong woman, no matter what you think about her actions."

On October 14, 2017, the largest-ever Mata Hari exhibition was opened in the Museum of Friesland in her hometown of Leeuwarden. Included in the exhibit are two of her personal scrapbooks and an oriental rug embroidered with the footsteps of her fan dance. Located in Margaretha's native town, the museum is well known for researching the life and career of Leeuwarden's world-famous citizen.

Her birthplace is located in the building at Kelders 33. The building suffered smoke and water damage during a fire in 2013 but was later restored. Architect Silvester Adema studied old drawings of the storefront to reconstruct it as it appeared when Adam Zelle, the father of Mata Hari, had a hat shop there.

In 1925, eight years after her execution, Monsieur Carlo Antoine's lawyers had the audacity to ask the court for the return of the three thousand francs paid Margaretha because of her lawsuit – even though he had never paid her a penny of the other five thousand francs awarded her. Their case was thrown out of court.

Margaretha wearing Jean Hallaure's uniform - 1910

To my darling Vadime
I am Marina, the most blissful of my identities.

235

Made in United States
Orlando, FL
01 December 2024

54738438R00134